The Kaiser's First POWs

The Kaiser's First POWs

Philip D. Chinnery

Pen & Sword
MILITARY

First published in Great Britain in 2018 by
Pen & Sword Military
An imprint of
Pen & Sword Books Ltd
47 Church Street
Barnsley
South Yorkshire
S70 2AS

Copyright © Philip Chinnery 2018

ISBN 978 1 47389 228 6

The right of Philip Chinnery to be identified as Author of this work
has been asserted by him in accordance with the Copyright, Designs and
Patents Act 1988.

A CIP catalogue record for this book is
available from the British Library.

Typeset by Aura Technology and Software Services, India
Printed and bound by CPI Group (UK) Ltd, Croydon, CR0 4YY

Pen & Sword Books Limited incorporates the imprints of Atlas, Archaeology,
Aviation, Discovery, Family History, Fiction, History, Maritime, Military,
Military Classics, Politics, Select, Transport, True Crime, Air World,
Frontline Publishing, Leo Cooper, Remember When, Seaforth Publishing,
The Praetorian Press, Wharncliffe Local History, Wharncliffe Transport,
Wharncliffe True Crime and White Owl.

For a complete list of Pen & Sword titles please contact
PEN & SWORD BOOKS LIMITED
47 Church Street, Barnsley, South Yorkshire, S70 2AS, England
E-mail: enquiries@pen-and-sword.co.uk
Website: www.pen-and-sword.co.uk

Contents

Introduction

The blazing inferno that became the First World War was sparked by an event that took place in Sarajevo on 28 June 1914. On that day Gavrilo Princip, a member of the Black Hand, a Serbian nationalist secret society, assassinated Archduke Franz Ferdinand, heir to the Austria-Hungarian throne. Shortly thereafter Austria-Hungary issued an ultimatum to Serbia, demanding that the assassins be brought to justice. Dissatisfied with the result, Austria-Hungary declared war on Serbia on 28 July 1914.

Serbia had Slavic ties to Russia, which began to mobilize its vast army. Germany was allied to Austria-Hungary by treaty and considered the Russian mobilization to be an act of war against Austria-Hungary, so declared war on Russia on 1 August.

France was bound by treaty to support Russia and declared war against Germany and Austria-Hungary on 3 August. On the following day German troops crossed the frontier into neutral Belgium. They were implementing the Schlieffen Plan, created in 1905 by the then German army chief of staff, Field Marshal Alfred von Schlieffen, which involved an advance into neutral Belgium before swinging south into France. This would avoid the fortifications along the French-German border and should lead to the defeat of France before Russia had time to mobilize her armed forces.

Britain had guaranteed Belgian independence in the Treaty of London 1839 and once that country was invaded by Germany, Britain declared war on 4 August and prepared to send the British Expeditionary Force (BEF) to support the French and Belgian forces now in contact with the German army.

Further afield, Japan, honouring a treaty with Britain, declared war on Germany on 23 August 1914. Italy was a friend of both Germany and Austria-Hungary, but remained neutral until she joined the British and French in May 1915. The United States would remain neutral until 1917 when President Wilson finally declared war on Germany on 6 April 1917.

Fortunately the Schlieffen Plan did not take into account the stiff resistance encountered in Belgium, nor the presence of the BEF, but it did result in the capture of tens of thousands of Belgian, French and British troops. Before the French could be subdued, Russia joined the war and the Germans found themselves fighting on two fronts. They were more than a match for the Russians, however, and great numbers of Russian prisoners would be taken at the Battle of Tannenberg in East Prussia. The Russians would become the largest single group of prisoners in the German prisoner of war system.

In September 1915 large numbers of Serbian prisoners began to arrive, following the Austro-German-Bulgarian invasion of that country. The Romanian government declared war on the Central Powers in August 1916, leading to the occupation of that kingdom and an influx of Romanian prisoners into Germany. (The countries referred to as the Central Powers were Austria, Hungary, Germany, Bulgaria and the Ottoman Empire.)

Vor dem Abmarsch

Captured Russian prisoners about to be marched away to a prison camp.

Italy had joined the war on the side of the Entente Cordiale, the alliance between France, Great Britain and Russia. They were soon under attack from Austro-Hungarian forces and when the Italian front collapsed as a result of the Battle of Caporetto in October to November 1917, large numbers of Italian prisoners began to appear in the German Empire. By the end of the war, the Germans had taken approximately 2.8 million prisoners of war. This book will describe the life and times of these prisoners and the manner in which the Germans dealt with the problems involved in accommodating them.

In 1915 the German government published a book in Berlin entitled *1915*. It was produced in an attempt to portray the Germans as a civilized people who were destined to win the war, but in the meantime they would treat their prisoners with care and compassion. The aim of this book is to compare *1915* to the reality of captivity, as experienced by the prisoners themselves. The book was translated into English by the German publisher and sections are reproduced here, word for word, with errors of spelling and grammar included to add to the authenticity. Personal accounts from former prisoners will describe the reality of falling into the hands of the German army and life as a prisoner of the Kaiser.

Philip D. Chinnery, London 2016

Chapter 1

The Horrors of War

Although the German invasion of neutral Belgium horrified the world, it was an important part of the Schlieffen Plan, designed to avoid the French fortifications along the French-German border. The Germans were confident that they could defeat the French quickly, but the Belgian army put up a stiff resistance, slowing the German advance and allowing the British Expeditionary Force to join the fight. As the British Tommies embarked for the continent, the mighty British Empire began to stir and Canadians, Australians and Indians also began to prepare to join the war.

Although Britain did not maintain a large standing army like France and Germany, it was highly professional as the Germans discovered to their cost when they first met the 80,000-strong BEF at Mons, a small Belgian town, on 23 August 1914. The BEF formed up on the left flank of the French army and although outnumbered by about three to one, they managed to withstand the advance of the German First Army for forty-eight hours. They prevented the Germans from outflanking the French army, but when the Frenchmen began to retreat, the British had little alternative but to fall back too. British casualties were recorded at just over 1,600 but they had inflicted three times as many casualties on the Germans.

The two corps of the BEF retreated for two more days until the II Corps commander, General Horace Smith-Dorrien decided to stop and fight. Although he was disobeying the orders of General Sir John French, the BEF commander, his men were exhausted and in low spirits. On the morning of 26 August they reached Le Cateau and began to dig in. They were at a disadvantage from the start due to lack of cover on the open ground, with the Germans advancing from the higher ground to the north. The men and artillery of the BEF were badly exposed and the heavy German guns caused significant losses among the defenders. By the time the battle was over, 7,812 men had been lost and thousands more were captured. Although the German advance had been halted for a while, General French was livid that Smith-Dorrien had disobeyed his orders and he was eventually relieved of his position on health grounds.

One of the prisoners taken that day was 42-year-old Major Yate of the 2nd Battalion, King's Own Yorkshire Light Infantry (KOYLI). He commanded one of the two companies that fought until all their officers had been killed or wounded and their ammunition was exhausted. Yate led his nineteen surviving infantrymen in a charge against the enemy and was taken prisoner. He was sent to Torgau prison camp, from where he escaped on 19 September. He was quickly apprehended by local workers who stopped him because of his unusual appearance and demanded to see inside his haversack. At this point he pulled out an open razor and cut his own throat rather than return to captivity. He was posthumously awarded the Victoria Cross on 2 August 1919.

The German army laid siege to the French forts at Maubeuge on 25 August 1914. Occupied by 47,000 French troops, the forts lay at the intersection of the Brussels and Liège railways that ran straight to Paris and were thus an important objective in the German Schlieffen Plan.

Regiments of German troops advance in open order across the fields of Belgium.

Major Yate of the 2nd Battalion, King's Own Yorkshire Light Infantry was taken prisoner and imprisoned in Torgau camp from which he later escaped. When he was recaptured he took his own life and was posthumously awarded the Victoria Cross.

On 29 August the Germans began a week-long bombardment of the forts and then attacked with 60,000 troops. On 7 September the defenders of the forts surrendered and 40,000 French prisoners were taken, along with several thousand allied stragglers who had sought refuge in the forts during the retreat.

The retreat continued until 5 September 1914, when a French counter-attack from Paris began. Six French field armies and the BEF advanced along the River Marne and forced the German army to retreat north-west, leading to the First Battle of the Aisne and the 'Race for the Sea'. Thereafter the conflict on the Western Front stagnated into trench warfare as both sides dug in for the duration.

Although trench warfare received most of the press during the war, the bloodiest phases were the short 'war of movement' at the beginning and the end of the war. The battles of August and September 1914 were responsible for nearly three-quarters of a million casualties. The French army suffered 330,000 casualties, including 80,000 dead, and the German casualties were almost as high at 300,000. The smaller British Expeditionary Force sustained around 30,000 casualties, nearly half its total strength.

A bullet struck Lieutenant Henderson in the head. It entered sideways between his eyebrows and came out beneath his temple. It broke all the bone along the forehead, ruined the sight of the right eye and paralysed his eyelids.

It was 8 November 1914 and he was fighting with his regiment, the Duke of Wellingtons, in front of Gheluvelt against a Prussian Guard regiment. They were 5 miles east of the Belgian town of Ypres and the Germans were determined to break through the British lines. His position was eventually overrun by the enemy who paused only to search through his pockets and steal everything of value. That night the temperature dropped down to freezing and he

A German painting of British and French prisoners taken at the fall of the fortresses at Maubeuge.

British troops leisurely advancing with full kit, apparently not under fire at this time.

The horrors of war: British dead awaiting burial.

crawled into a dugout for shelter. He remained there for three long days, drifting in and out of consciousness.

On the morning of 11 November a German infantryman discovered him and together with a comrade they lifted him out of the dugout and began to carry the wounded officer to the rear of the lines. They had not gone more than a kilometre when they met a German doctor. Henderson later recalled:

> On seeing me he remarked '*Ah, Englander!*' and held a revolver to my head whilst he cursed me in German. The only word I understood was '*Swine-hund*' frequently repeated. Finally the sentry spoke to him, and after a heated discussion with him, he took me by the shoulder and gave me a kick, which sent me staggering down the road. The sentry picked me up and we went on to a cottage, where there was a second doctor, who bound my wound, gave me half a cup of water and sent me on. A little further down the road an unter-officer jumped off a wagon, followed me for a good mile jeering at me; having spat at me, he then left me.

Further down the road Henderson came upon a company of German soldiers having water served out to them. He asked their officer if he could have a drink, but he was ignored. One of the soldiers handed him his water bottle, whereupon the officer cursed him so loudly that the startled soldier snatched the bottle back and made himself scarce.

When Henderson finally reached the field hospital he met a dozen wounded men from his regiment. The German doctors re-dressed their wounds and they were directed to an open yard where they sat until nightfall. At dusk the rain began to fall and as the weary men were roused to their feet it began to pour down. The band of prisoners was surrounded by infantry and then a ring of lance-carrying cavalrymen – Uhlans, who used their horses to tread on the heels of the prisoners – to hurry them along. Despite their wounds, the prisoners were ordered to carry the Germans' packs as they began a miserable march to their next destination. Three hours and 18 kilometres later they arrived at Tourcoing, where they were put into a theatre where they spent the night laying on some straw and shivering from the wet and cold.

The following day Henderson discovered just how cruel his captors could be to their wounded prisoners. In the morning they were marched to the local train station and while they were waiting Henderson lay down on the platform. A German officer appeared with his bulldog, which proceeded to lick Henderson's face. The officer then kicked the dog while making derogatory remarks about the *Englander* to the German soldiers waiting nearby. Finally a train arrived and Henderson was put into a third-class compartment, where he lay down on the wooden floor. A fellow officer from his regiment, Lieutenant Bennett, was put into the same carriage. He gave Henderson his greatcoat and put his cap under his head to try to protect his head wound from the jolting of the train.

The journey was to take four days and on the way they stopped at Münster for food. There were some French officers on the train and the Germans took them away to a buffet for a good meal. However, Henderson and his fellow officer were told to sit with the French other ranks and eat their food out of tin basins. It was becoming clear that the British were to receive worse treatment than their French or Belgian allies. The French were allowed to purchase soda water at the station but the sentries refused the request from the British officers, stating 'Nothing for the *Englander*'.

Captured British troops searching the dead for personal possessions.

At another station Henderson was taken to a Red Cross room where his casualty card was inspected by a doctor. The doctor said that it was too soon to re-dress his wound, gave him an aspirin and sent him back to his carriage.

On 14 November the train pulled into Osnabrück station in the north of Germany and the prisoners were marched off to the nearby prisoner-of-war camp in an old artillery barracks. On arrival they were ordered to turn out their pockets, whereupon Henderson handed over a pair of spectacles and a broken pencil. The German NCO indignantly asked for the rest of his possessions and refused to believe him when he said that they had already been taken from him when he was wounded. He had to remove his boots and puttees to prove that he was not hiding anything of value, and was then led to a room where the camp doctor worked for two or three days a week. The doctor simply put a fresh piece of bandage over the wound and told the sentry to escort the officer to a room that already housed ten Russian and two French officers.

The lack of treatment for Henderson's wound was fast becoming critical. He could not sleep at all due to the effects of his injury and would lie awake all night listening to the hours strike and watching daylight arrive through the windows. A Russian who slept opposite him used to stand at the foot of his bed for ten minutes first thing every morning and last thing every night. When Henderson finally asked him why he did it, he replied: 'Oh, when they brought you in here I was sure you were dying, and I came to see every day whether you would last the night out.'

By the end of the first week, the right side of Henderson's face was turning green and blue and he could not bite into a piece of bread properly. It felt as if his gums were allowing his teeth to turn sideways. The German doctor was of no help, so Henderson turned to Dr Housey, a Belgian doctor who was also a prisoner. He looked at the wound and told Henderson that he had arrived just in time because he had gangrene. Fortunately Dr Housey was able to clean the wound two or three times a day using a syringe and hydrogen peroxide. For three months his right eyelid was closed and paralysed, but in January it starting quivering and within a couple of weeks he could open and shut it. However, he still could not see anything out of that eye.

The rations supplied by the Germans were totally inadequate for a wounded man: breakfast usually comprised acorn coffee and a small roll of bread (no sugar or butter); lunch was a watery soup with a small piece of meat or potato and sometimes rice; dinner was acorn coffee and another small roll. The Germans would not advance the officers any money to buy extra provisions, so for the time being they had to survive on basic prisoners' rations.

Three more months passed and then one day Henderson was sent to see an oculist, who was the regimental doctor at a nearby barracks. He examined Henderson and then informed him that the optical nerve had been severed and he would not be able to see out of that eye again. Over the coming months a number of prisoner-of-war doctors took charge of Henderson, one of them informing him that if had been operated on earlier, his wound would have healed within two months. As it was, thirteen months later his wound had still not closed up properly and he was still removing splinters of bone from his shattered forehead with a pair of scissors.

Lieutenant R.V. Gracey was serving with the 14th Battalion, Royal Irish Rifles when he was wounded in the third German line by a hand grenade around 5 pm on 1 July 1916. This was north-west of Thiepval, on the road from Thiepval to Grandcourt. He was hit in both feet and legs, and spent the night lying in a hole on the battlefield waiting for help to arrive. In the morning he started to crawl towards a dead soldier nearby and tried to get his water bottle. However, a German sniper was watching and fired at him twice, forcing him back into the hole. The sniper must have seen that Gracey was wounded, as he could not let his feet touch the ground. The following morning the Germans came out and carried him back to their trenches in an oil sheet suspended from a pole. The occupants of the trenches were Saxons and they treated him well, giving him coffee and bread. One of them tried to bandage his wounds with field dressings. They were curious as to what he thought of the Zeppelin raids on London, which they thought had been a great success. Stretcher-bearers then carried him to a dugout and from it to the Grandcourt dressing station. On the way they stopped for a break in a village where Gracey was again given coffee.

At the dressing station orderlies brought water or coffee to both their own and the English wounded. Gracey's wounds were dressed on 4 July, three days after he had been wounded. There were around 120 men lying on stretchers, roughly half British and half German. The German doctor on duty was very busy, but the German padre there was very kind to the wounded.

Two days later Gracey was carried by ambulance to the grounds of a château where mixed German and British wounded were placed on straw in the open and given some coffee. During the night it rained heavily and the German wounded were moved inside a large marquee. However, the British were left outside in the rain and most of them became wet through.

The next day Gracey was taken to St. Quentin and placed in a large room in a house along with a dozen other British officers. He would be there until 15 July. The food was sufficient

British troops about to go 'over the top' as shells burst ahead of them.

to preserve life: coffee and bread in the morning; soup in the middle of the day; bread and tea without milk around 6 pm. The German nursing sisters were very kind and helped the bad cases to wash their hands and faces every morning. However, conditions were very bad with only two German doctors and four nurses to tend to the hundreds of British wounded in the house and a nearby church. The medical arrangements were totally inadequate and many men received no dressings for their wounds for a fortnight. Gracey was given two dressings by pointing out to the doctor the swellings in both groins and he was given an injection for tetanus around 8 July. Many of the men received no dressings at all within a fortnight. Although the Germans were willing, the medical arrangements were tragically inadequate.

Despite the fact that they were all confined to bed in the officers' room, the town commandant informed the German doctor that they were trying to communicate from the windows with the French civilians. As a result, all the windows were nailed shut and painted white up to the top; no fresh air was allowed, only via the door open to the staircase. As the weather was very hot they protested strongly against the accusation of the town commandant but the doctor said that he was powerless.

At St. Quentin they were interviewed individually by a very clever German who spoke English and French perfectly. The officers only gave their name, rank and regiment. At this time all notebooks etc. were collected for inspection. Fortunately Gracey had destroyed his maps and notebook soon after capture.

On 15 July Gracey was put on a hospital train from St. Quentin to Ohrdruf in Saxony. They were given enough food and the Red Cross orderlies were attentive. By food, this meant black bread and coffee. Some of the officers in a worse condition were given wine. These included Gracey, who by now was feverish and his feet had started to swell. The whole train smelled of dried blood and unwashed wounds.

Upon arrival at Ohrdruf hospital Gracey was put in the charge of French doctors, who were very considerate and his dressings were changed frequently. However, the treatment arrived too late as the infection had spread from his feet up to his groin and his right foot gave him intense pain. On 23 July he was put in the care of Dr Stern, the German surgeon.

The men were put on a Form II diet, which consisted of bread and dreadful coffee at 7.30 am; beef tea which made them sick and had to be given up at 9.30 am. Soup followed at 11 am, followed by a minute quantity of stewed fruit; soup again at 6 pm with a little mashed potato. Fish was supplied with potatoes twice a week, but they had to stop eating it as it was bad.

Gracey's condition continued to worsen and his right foot was amputated on 11 August. All Dr Stern's patients, when lucky enough to get a dressing, had to be carried by French orderlies on a stretcher for a distance of 400 to 500 yards to his operating room in another building and back again, no matter what their condition or what weather conditions prevailed. Of the six officers, two had amputations; one had an amputation and a very large wound in his back; one was hit in the lungs; one had a broken leg; and the other had been badly wounded by a trench mortar.

Captain H. Master of the 2nd Queen's Regiment was hit in the leg during the retreat of his company outside the village of Ledeghem. He lay in a turnip field until the firing died down and some Belgian peasants carried him into their cottage and gave him some coffee to drink. He was discovered by a German patrol two days later and taken to a house that was being used as a hospital for German soldiers wounded in the First Battle of Ypres. The German doctor treated him quite well and set and bandaged his broken leg and for two days he lay in a room being fed twice a day with soup and bread. On the third day he was taken to a train station with a score of wounded German soldiers. They lay outside on straw for two hours while waiting for the train. It was bitterly cold and Master discovered first-hand what German soldiers could be like. He later wrote: 'They shouted, calling me names, threatened me with fixed bayonets, and loaded and pointed their rifles at me. This went on for some ten minutes until I managed to attract the attention of a German officer who put a stop to it.'

Master spent three days on the train, lying on the packed floor with the German wounded. At the larger stations the German wounded were given cigarettes and food and at Cologne Red Cross women came in and washed the men, but the treatment did not extend to the wounded officer.

Things started to improve when Master was carried on a stretcher to a private house in Münster that was being used as a hospital. The house was being kept by two old German baronesses – Baronin Louise Von Gerssdorff and Baronin Else Von Ardenne – who practically treated him as their guest. He was supplied with library books and copies of the *Daily Mail*, obtained through the Dutch consul. However, his leg had been badly set and walking on crutches was an ordeal, but regardless he was soon on his way to a prisoner-of-war camp in Mainz, a fortified cathedral town on the River Rhine, with a population of around 110,000. The camp barracks were on a hill in the middle of the town overlooking the valley of the Rhine with extensive views and up to 700 officers could be accommodated there.

Captain Master was put in a room with ten French officers. They had iron beds with straw mattresses and a hard chair each to sit on and just two lamps between the lot of them. Apart from 30 English officers, there were also 150 French and 150 Russian and all shared an exercise ground 50 yards x 50 yards surrounded on three sides by an 8ft barbed-wire fence. The area

Prisoners of war taken at Arras in May 1917 pose for the photographer from their train carriage, usually used for carrying horses.

was so small that they had to exercise in two parties with allocated times for the compulsory exercise; the rest of the time they had to stay in their barracks.

Every three months the rooms were searched in a very thorough manner. An officer and eight soldiers would search every room: bedclothes, cupboards and mattresses as well as the clothes the prisoners were wearing. Articles such as penknives, razors and coins were confiscated.

During the first three months in the camp the discipline was very harsh, although fortunately the officer in charge of Master's barracks was of a more kindly nature. The commanding officer had also made himself very unpopular and unpleasant and complaints were made to the Spanish consul when he visited the camp. Soon after, things began to improve and the commanding officer was replaced.

In April 1915 Master and some of the other officers were transferred to Friedberg camp, about 25 miles north of Frankfurt. The town was quite small with a population of less than 10,000 and the officer prisoners were quartered in a stone barracks on the extreme outskirts of the town. Master found himself sharing a room with seven French and one English officer. The Germans insisted on mixing the nationalities and at that time a maximum of two English officers could be allowed in a room. Master later reported to the War Office:

In cases of some officers, who were badly wounded and who had been ill-fed in their hospital, coming to a camp where the food was also not good, they were unable to regain their health. This resulted in running wounds, extending over many months. During my year at Friedberg we had the same commandant, although we had no direct dealings with him. Requests were made through the German officer in charge of the barrack, and for the first six months we had a very pleasant officer over us. He happened to be a wealthy and influential man, and in many cases he forced the commandant to give way to our requests. When he left we were all sorry. Captain Sturt then took charge. He liked the English and hated the French. He spoke English perfectly, his father being English, who had become a naturalised German. He also tried to help us, but his influence with the commandant was nil, and many petty changes now came about. Personally, Captain Sturt tried to do what he could for me. I was given extra coal on my asking him, and when my motor papers, which I received from home, were prohibited, he allowed me to come along to his office and read them there. He also took us on long and interesting walks. The German officers here in this camp were a very different stamp to those at Mainz. They did what they could to make our confinement as easy as possible, but were hampered by many rules and regulations which came direct from the authorities in Berlin. A rumour which had been circulated for some time was confirmed at the end of May. I was among the first lot of officers to be exchanged to Chateau d'Oex in Switzerland.

Corporal Patrick Durham of the 10th Battalion, Australian Imperial Force (AIF) was wounded at the end of August 1916. During the fighting around Moquet Farm near Pozières (Somme) he found himself in a shell crater with his platoon sergeant and half a dozen wounded comrades. Sergeant Badger had also been wounded and it was clear that they were not going to achieve their objective. When Sergeant Badger was hit again – a nasty wound in the groin – Durham decided to try to reach friendly lines, leaving the sergeant in charge of the other men. He managed to crawl for 200 yards before he was hit in the leg and fell into a shell crater where two or three other wounded lay. He was bleeding very badly and the nerves to one of his feet had been severed, but one of the wounded tied a bandage around his leg and he continued crawling towards the rear. Finally, exhaustion overtook him and as darkness fell he tumbled into another shell crater.

Soon thereafter some unwounded men joined Durham, with the news that Sergeant Badger had died from his wounds and that the Germans had retaken the trench that the Aussies had thrown them out of earlier. They were now surrounded. During the night the unwounded men left to try to find a way through to their own lines and other wounded men joined Durham in the shell crater. As a drizzling rain began to fall, Durham fainted from loss of blood and awoke at dawn to find a German patrol pointing their rifles at him. They were lucky because the Germans saw that they were wounded and started to carry the men back to their lines. He remained there until the next evening when he was carried under shellfire about a mile to a dressing station where his wounds were bandaged. He stayed there for a couple of hours before a motor ambulance took him to a nearby railway station from where he was taken to a place called Courtrai and a hospital in an old lace factory.

Durham later wrote in his diary:

There proved to be quite a number of Australian and British wounded here, some of the poor chaps being badly knocked about. This hospital is well fitted out and our chaps get every attention. There being no difference whether one is English or German. They both get the same treatment. The food, although there is no luxuries, is plain, but good and nutritious. I went under the X-ray today after I had been dressed. My leg is very painful

British prisoners of war being escorted away from the front lines in 1916. (*Australian War Memorial*)

and sleep is impossible. About the 29th August they operated on me and took out some bone splinters. Two weeks later they put me on a train to Germany.

For further information on Durham, see Chapter 6 (Sanitary Arrangements and Care of the Sick).

Another Australian taken prisoner at Mouquet Farm was an unnamed officer who was severely wounded in the head and had to endure two years of imprisonment before he was eventually repatriated via neutral Holland. He later wrote an account of his experiences:

I had received a piece of either shrapnel or bomb in the left hip and was then shot through the head while behind a boulder. The bullet had entered my head about half an inch to the right of my right eye, passed through my head and emerged under my left ear. I lay there for some time, and remember calling out, 'Are there any Australians near?' 'Yes' came a reply from about ten yards to the rear. I immediately scrambled up and dashed into a shell-hole, where two of our lads were lying, one of whom was also wounded. As I stumbled into this shell-hole I received another wound in the left side from a bullet. We lay in that shell-hole until dark. I was completely blind in my right eye and could hardly see out of my left eye.

We wandered about for days in 'No Man's Land', hiding during the daytime and trying to find our way back to our trenches at night. The ground was muddy, and covered with an unyielding undergrowth of thistles, which cruelly lacerated our hands whilst attempting to crawl through. We could hear Germans talking on every side of us. When we advanced in this painful fashion for about 300 yards we heard a large party of Germans approaching along some sort of communication trench. The enemy party set to work to deepen the trench, which lay just a few yards in front of us. After they had been working for an hour, our artillery suddenly opened fire upon them. A German officer and two German soldiers immediately jumped into the shell-hole in which we were hiding. This ended it. At first the Germans were just as amazed and dumbfounded as we were; but as soon as the German officer realised how matters stood, I and my two comrades became his prisoners of war.

We were taken into the trench, and kept there till dawn. I asked to have my wounds bandaged, and this was attended to. My wounds were dressed and bandaged by a German medical man, who was palpably very nervous and thoroughly unstrung. While my wounds were being dressed the trench was under our own artillery fire, and the Germans were literally squealing. They jumped into any positions of shelter or vantage that offered. A German officer tossed me out of the corner in which I had taken refuge and got into it himself. I hardly blamed him for that. At dawn we were marched along trenches, a distance of 7 or 8 kilometres to the rear of the enemy lines. The trenches were veritable mud channels, and in our weak and wounded condition we found this tramp a very trying ordeal. In the trenches the Germans gave us some coffee, and I remember them offering me some biscuits, but I could not open my mouth to eat them. They took us back to company head-quarters. There my head wound was cleansed and rebandaged. Struggling along the muddy trenches to company headquarters a German officer lent me his stick; he himself picked up a shovel. I thought this rather an act of decency. I have no complaint to make of our treatment by the Germans while in the lines.

We were subjected to a rigorous cross-examination at head-quarters of the company. Later on we were moved to divisional head-quarters at Bertincourt, and again industriously and ingeniously interrogated. Of course, the Germans gained no information from us beyond our names and regimental particulars. Back here there were a number of British and Australian prisoners of war, but I seemed to be the only officer. All the wounded here were given an anti-tetanus injection. We were then taken in old wagons about 15 kilometres to what appeared to be a clearing station.

We had been captured around 2 am and at about 6 pm I was taken into a church. It was filled with badly-wounded German soldiers. It was a veritable chamber of horrors, and gave me a grotesque idea of what Dante may have imagined when he penned his poem *Inferno*. Here having first been given a cup of coffee substitute (ersatz), I was ordered to bed. The doctor who examined my wounds said, in broken English, 'It is a pity the German soldier was not a better shot.' Precisely what he meant by this I have never bothered to find out.

I received no more food or drink before being taken away, on the night of 29th August, to Velu. The camp consisted of tents erected outside an old chateau. We lay on straw, and had our wounds attended to. Furthermore, we were given soup, bread and jam, and 'coffee'. At the end of about the third day of our stay at Velu we were put on a train. We were absolutely crawling with vermin, picked up from the filthy straw and blankets. Officers and men prisoners of war were packed into the guard's van to lie upon shavings; the German wounded rode in the carriage. We were all badly wounded, and this nine hours' railway 'jaunt' proved a very trying journey indeed for us.

Eventually we arrived at Caudry, where we were placed in hospital, all our clothing having been taken away from us. We were put to bed in a German ward. Here we were fairly well attended to. A German nursing sister wrote letters for a couple of English prisoners of war whose wounds would not permit them to write their own home letters. But, after about four days in this ward, we were moved into a ward that was 'all British'. Here beds were hard, the food was curtailed, and the medical attention became slacker than had been the case in the ward we had just left. So negligent was the medical attention that the wounds of some of the prisoners of war in this ward were crawling with maggots, which also overran the bedding. To insure [sic] your wounds being dressed at all, it was necessary to pull the bandages wholly off your wounds. Several wounded prisoners of war died while I was here, but I do not think any of these were Australians. There were fully 100 Australian prisoners of war in this hospital, nearly all of them in this ward.

Somewhere between the 10th and 12th of September we were transferred to Grafenwohr, in Bavaria. In the party there were about 70 Australian prisoners of war. When we arrived at Grafenwohr, those like myself who could do so had to walk two miles to the hospital on the outskirts of the town. Those wounded in the legs were lumbered to hospital in lorries minus springs, and had the most trying of rough rides. From Grafenwohr I was removed to the Danube fortress of Ingoldstadt. Here we were made to walk about eight kilometres to the camp, where we arrived thoroughly exhausted, but were cordially received by British officer prisoners of war who were already quartered there.

A column of British prisoners having been relieved of their equipment after capture. Note that none of them are carrying water bottles.

Time passed slowly while the wounded officer waited to see if he would be repatriated. He spent four weeks in Constance, waiting for an examination by a medical commission, but was then returned to Germany. Eventually he was moved to Ströhen, near Hannover on 25 May 1917 and stayed there until 23 January 1918. He later recalled:

> The treatment here was nothing short of frightful. Prison life was one continuous 'strafe' (punishment). The food was impossible to live upon, in fact it was not fit for pigs. Several officers were bayonetted within the camp upon the most trivial pretext. The 'jugs' or 'clinks' were always full. The notorious Hun bully, Niemeyer, was commandant here for a time. We had other notorious 'strafe merchants' at the same camp. We were subjected to continuous irritating 'searches'. In short, of this camp it may justly be said that there was nothing good and everything was bad. Our own food issue was frequently stopped here, when we had to manage somehow to subsist on the German ration, and consequently almost starved. A fair-sized book could be written upon the iniquities and shortcomings of this German prison camp alone. There was scarcely any fuel issued during the most rigorous of winters.

Eventually he was moved to Bad Colberg where he found good quarters but a camp spoiled by a bad commandant. After he left for repatriation, two British officers were shot dead while trying to escape. However, he was now on his way home and spent eighteen days waiting in Aachen before he was sent across the border into Holland on 8 April 1918.

Chapter 2

Into the Bag: The First Prisoners

The German side of the story:

At the time of our going to press (1915) there were approximately one and a half million prisoners of war within the German Empire. If it is remembered, that besides these, numerous enemy soldiers were taken prisoners by the German troops during the fighting in Galicia and Serbia, who remained in Austria-Hungary, we come to numbers and figures, which will withstand all detractor efforts of our enemies. The prisoners of war within Germany, now already, represent twice as large a number of men, as the peace footing of the powerful German army calls for, four times as many as were opposed to each other in the greatest battle of all ages, the nation's battle at Leipzig.

A million hands are required for providing housing, food, clothing and catering for our unbidden guests, for nursing the wounded and sick amongst them, and for dealing with the vast railway, postal and parcel service resulting from their presence. And as the German nation is, at the same time, by carrying on the greatest and most ferocious war of all ages, by feeding many millions of warriors, by manufacturing the required munitions, being entirely cut off from imports from abroad, achieving enormous tasks, it is obvious what economic task it is to house and feed these prisoners of war.

At our times, where million and milliard are everyday words, it is often difficult to figure before one's mind's eye, what such figures mean. Looking at our first illustration one might believe to be regarding a picture from the densely populated Russia, and yet there are only

Russian prisoners taken by the Austrian army in 1915. Note the youngsters at the front.

Hungry British prisoners waiting to receive their rations from a German field kitchen.

500 Russian prisoners of war before us. The second illustration seems to be a pretty large collection of Oriental types, and yet there are but a few hundred Turcos, Zouaves, Indians and other Mahomedans, listening to a discourse being held in their camp. The next picture shows us a large number of French prisoners from the Regensburg camp, the following one group from the Czersk camp. The prisoners of war in Nurnberg are just lined up for the roll call. Upon notice being given that a photograph is to be taken, a couple of hundred Russian prisoners of war in Görlitz hurry to place themselves in front of the camera. The following picture illustrates camp life at Soltau. But at each time, there are only a few hundred men before us, and when, again and again, in the 150 large camps, in the 500 smaller workers' camps and at the many thousand places where prisoners are employed at work, one receives the same impression of the enormous numbers of enemies taken prisoners of war, one might imagine hearing the tread of a new migration of peoples, witnessing the dawn of a new age, in which millions of brave German fighters cross the narrow boundaries, in order to teach the world the respect due to German energy, and have forced one and a half million men to enter the German Empire as prisoners of war. When, some day, these return home, they may, on the Volga and in Siberia, on the Pyrenees, in the Scotch mountains, on the Atlas, in India, Australia and Canada deliver the message, that they have experienced the Kaiser's word, what it means to attack Germany, and that, during their captivity, they have had an opportunity of seeing what the 'Kultur' and order of these 'German Huns' are. Even in the small workers' camps, such as Wittorferfeld in Holstein, and Weitmoos on the Chiem Lake in Bavaria there is the same imposing aspect of the enormous number of prisoners of war; and yet, each time, it is only a small fraction of the total number, which one beholds.

In an attempt to illustrate the huge numbers of prisoners in their hands, 500 of the Russian prisoners at Guben camp have been assembled, with guards in their dark uniforms in the front row.

This appears to be a huge number of prisoners but there are only a few hundred Turcos, Zouaves, Indians and other Mohammedan prisoners in this camp at Wünsdorf, being addressed by an interpreter.

Prisoners of various nationalities, but mostly French, gather in the courtyard of the camp at Regensburg.

Russian prisoners in the camp at Czersk.

The residents of the camp at Nürnberg assemble in ranks for roll-call.

Large numbers of Russian prisoners are assembled for this photo at Görlitz.

Camp life at Soltau with guards and officers in the group at the front.

One of the smaller work camps at Wittorferfeld in Holstein.

Prisoners prepare to leave the camp at Weitmoos on the Chiem Lake in Bavaria. These working parties would work in the local area on farms, forests, quarries, etc.

But not only soldiers, taken prisoners of war had to be interned in the German concentration camps, also numerous persons liable or eligible for service in the enemies' armies, persons suspect of espionage, and last of all, inhabitants of the occupied districts for sake of their own safety, had to be interned for a more or less long period. In our views we see male prisoners from the prisoners' camp at Traunstein, women and children from the concentration camp at Holzminden, the lot of whom the Army Board is endeavouring, to alleviate in every possible manner.

What this enormous number of prisoners means, will be evident from the calculation that if these one and a half million men were made to cross the German frontier, four abreast, on their return home, it would require no less than 250 hours for their exit. What it means to cater for the absolute necessities only, for such a number of men is obvious from the fact that one single meal of 1.25 liters (2.5 pints) per head for one and a half million men will represent a load, that it will take six railway trains at 30 cars each to convey, and such a vast volume of food has to be procured and prepared, day for day and month after month.

But the authorities were not satisfied with concentrating the enemy prisoners in camps, in guarding and sustaining them, they also sought to occupy them in a useful manner, and, at the same time, to save them from ennui and melancholy by entertainments, sports and games, to provide them with spiritual blessing and solace of their respective religions, to enable them to communicate with their homes by mail and parcel post, and, lastly, to afford to such who so desired, the opportunity and means of improving their knowledge

Male civilian internees held captive at Traunstein.

Washday at Holzminden internees' camp.

and skill. And that at this advent of hundreds of thousands of members of almost all races in the world no serious, fatal epidemics have been spread, is solely due to medical science, which achieved almost miracles in disinfection, vaccination and prophylactics.

The same as the tales of the atrocities committed by German soldiers, of the warlike spirit of the German nation and the innumerable fables told in the press abroad in disfavour of Germany, also the repeated reports on the bad treatment of the prisoners of

Children were also interned with their parents in Holzminden camp.

war in Germany are untrue. No one will be surprised, if the German 'Landsturm' man did, at first, not show a very friendly mien towards the Cossacks, who had destroyed and pillaged the flourishing province of East Prussia, had quite unnecessarily burnt cottage and farm, tortured and murdered the defenceless, carried off women and children. It was only too natural that vexation was felt towards England, who for years had planned the isolation of Germany, and had, without any true cause, joined the enemies of Germany. Just as plausible it is that Senegal negroes, Gurkhas, Tartars and Calmoucks, to the bloodthirsty savagery of whom so many a German soldier had fallen a victim, were not regarded with over-amorous eyes. But German generosity and German kindheartedness soon broke the crust, and as the following chapters and our illustrations will show, everything was done, that was possible in the present hard times of war, to alleviate the lot of the prisoners of war and to inspire them with respect for German culture.

Tannenberg

In an attempt to relieve the pressure on the Belgians, French and British on the Western Front, the Russians invaded East Prussia in August 1914. Two Russian armies under Generals Rennenkampf and Samsonov were to attack the German Eighth Army commanded by Prittwitz. Rennenkampf began his advance on 20 August at Gumbinnen and defeated eight divisions of Germans, while Samsonov moved his Second Army southwards to threaten the German rear, defended by only three divisions.

The Germans luckily intercepted an uncoded Russian message, which indicated that Rennenkampf was in no hurry to advance further and by now there was a gap of 50 miles between the two Russian armies. On 23 August Prittwitz was replaced by General Von

Russian troops fleeing after their defeat at Tannenberg as pictured by a German artist.

Hindenburg, but his chief of staff Ludendorff confirmed his plan to attack the left flank of Samsonov's army. Gambling that Rennenkampf would be slow to continue his advance, Ludendorff moved three more divisions from Gumbinnen to bring his force up to six divisions and sent other troops to threaten Samsonov's right flank, leaving only a cavalry screen against Rennenkampf.

Samsonov's Second Army was advancing slowly along a 60-mile front when Ludendorff launched his attack on 26 August. His six divisions attacked Samsonov's left wing near Usdau and the heavy German artillery forced the Russians to retreat towards Neidenburg, pursued by the German infantry. Despite a Russian counter-attack from Soldau that enabled two Russian army corps to escape to the south-east, by nightfall on 29 August three Russian army corps were surrounded.

The Russians surrendered in their thousands and General Samsonov, lost in the surrounding forests with his aides, shot himself rather than follow his men into captivity. By the end of the month the Germans had taken 92,000 prisoners; an estimated 30,000 were killed or wounded and of the original 150,000 men, only around 10,000 escaped. Once further reinforcements had arrived, the Germans turned on Rennenkampf's First Army and drove it from East Prussia. In total the Russians lost around 250,000 men; an entire army, as well as huge amounts of equipment. It was no consolation, but by diverting German divisions from the advance into France, it allowed the French to regroup and counter-attack at the Marne.

Hindenburg and Ludendorff were fêted as heroes back in Germany. Hindenburg would later replace Erich von Falkenhayn as German army chief of staff, taking Ludendorff to Berlin with him as his quartermaster general.

Kriegsgefangene Schottländer in ihrer Nationaltracht

Scottish prisoners waiting by a train to take them to a prisoner-of-war camp. The Germans were amused by the kilts worn by Scottish soldiers.

Eight Horses or Forty Men

On the Western Front, the prisoners both fit and healthy were transported to Germany by train. For the officers it was usually in second-class carriages; for the men and the wounded it was cattle-class, in wagons marked '8 horses or 40 men'.

A number of common themes run through all the experiences of the prisoners: the wounded received little or no medical treatment; very little water or food was given to the British prisoners; the German Red Cross 'ladies' usually found at the railway stations to supply refreshments to the troops passing through refused to give food, water or help to the British prisoners. The trains would stop at every station where crowds of unruly civilians or soldiers would shout or spit at the prisoners.

The Germans had also got it into their heads that the regulation British soldier's clasp knife was being used to blind captured German soldiers. This particular type of knife had a marlin spike as well as a blade and the spike was used for removing stones from horses' hooves. In addition the Germans appear to have discovered 'dum dum' bullets (hollow-point bullets produced at the British arsenal in Dum Dum, near Calcutta) in the possession of some British soldiers. These are bullets that have had a part of the sharp end of the bullet cut or ground away, causing the bullet to expand and cause massive injuries upon impact. Whether or not this was ever proven, it was rumoured that some hundreds of British prisoners had been shot in retaliation.

Sergeant R. Gilling of the Scots Greys provides a good insight into the treatment of wounded British prisoners while they were being collected for shipment to Germany:

On the 14th September I and three other men were removed to Mons Station by light railway, where also were collected from 350 to 400 other British wounded from various villages round about Mons. The moment we arrived at Mons we all were taken into the station, where two trainloads of German cavalry had just arrived. These troops were drawn up in two lines; we were made to march through the lines, and were subjected to gross insults and ill-treatment. Curses were hurled at us, the men spat on us and kicked us, we were struck with sabres and bayonets, and Germans were not particular as to whether flesh wounds were inflicted or not; men with walking sticks had these snatched from them and were beaten with them; very many men with crutches had these kicked from under their arms, and when patients fell the crutches were used to beat them with. During this episode German officers and NCOs were with their men, and they, far from discouraging their men, encouraged them, even to the extent of cursing us in German and English and in taking part in these cowardly assaults. The officers were not young officers, but I saw many captains.

On conclusion of this parade we were marched into one large waiting room. There we were stripped and thoroughly searched. Every document, except our field service pay books, were taken away, also all knives, razors, needles, pins – in fact anything which in any way could serve as a weapon. The whole of our money was forcibly stolen and all our greatcoats were taken, except that of Company Sergeant-Major Thomas Denton, 2nd Duke of Wellingtons (West Riding) Regiment, who was very badly wounded in the leg, with bullets still in his leg, on which he had been kicked by a German, badly lacerating all the flesh on his calf. We spent the night in this waiting room without food or covering and were not permitted to leave the room for purposes of nature. Some 350 to 400 men

A collecting-point for British prisoners, probably some way behind the front lines.

were in this room, all windows and doors were shut, and we had barely standing room. At 4 am on 15th September a Feldwebel came in and shouted at us, and we realised he meant us to march out. This we did, and entered our train, where we were herded 55-65 men in each cattle truck – six in all. These trucks had evidently brought the cavalry we had met the previous evening, as the floors were still covered with several feet of fresh horse dung.

Sergeant Gilling's destination was Osnabrück, in the north of Germany. A town of some 65,000 occupants, situated on the River Hase, it was the centre of extensive ironworks. The prisoners were quartered in an artillery barracks, with the riding stable used as a concert room and even tennis courts in the yard. Interestingly, the author was stationed at the Kaiser Wilhelm Barracks in Osnabrück in the mid-1970s and it could hardly have changed, despite two world wars. Even the rifle racks were still present, set in the walls outside the barrack rooms.

Captain Beaman of the Royal Army Medical Corps (RAMC) was on a train en route from Mons to Torgau on 2 September 1914:

We arrived at Aachen at 6 pm and here a mob of drunken Uhlans (lancers) and railway employees were incited by a German Colonel to take us out of our carriage. He said it was scandalous that we, who had gouged out the eyes of German wounded with the marlin spikes of our clasp knives, should travel in a second-class carriage, while German wounded were in cattle trucks. Several of the mob had these English clasp-knives and were threatening to practise upon us, some tried to hit us through the windows, and some were making efforts to get into the corridor when a young officer came up and quelled them.

The howl of an angry mob is most unpleasant and terrifying. I for one never wish to hear it again, the song of the shell is far preferable. We were now given a special guard, who were very much suspicious and stand-offish at first, but rapidly thawed. We owe this guard much, for by their kind offices we obtained some food. The German Red Cross gave no food to prisoners, wounded or otherwise. At times it is shown to them and then withdrawn, with kindly remarks that it is not for swine.

We were visited by a German officer, and complaints were made of our treatment and a demand made to see the German commandant or the American Consul at Cologne. We were informed that there were various charges against us, and that we should be searched and examined later.

At about 6 pm on the 3rd we arrived at Dortmund, and under a very heavy guard we were marched to the Station Kommandantur. Here our Senior Medical Officer had an interview with the commandant, who was very polite and accepted our word that all charges of ill-treatment of German wounded were false, and further ordered the Red Cross to give us food. This they did very unwillingly. One lady when asked if she could speak English, replied, 'I can, but I won't.' After our meal our journey recommenced, but under better conditions. The guard protected us from insults, and we were allowed to buy a meal at Kriesen about 9 pm, the first meal we had had since Bavai three days earlier. We arrived at Torgau about 1 pm after nearly 80 hours in the train.

Torgau was a town on the River Elbe, with a population of around 15,000. The fourteen British medical officers on the train joined other officers in Fort Zinna and in the old Brückenkopf

Barracks, built close to the river. This prisoner-of-war camp was under the jurisdiction of the 4th Army Corps.

The abuse of the British prisoners was often orchestrated by the German officers, presumably for propaganda reasons. However, the average German soldier was often not so unsympathetic; maybe he thought that perhaps he might be wounded and a prisoner himself one day. Captain E.E. Orford of the Suffolk Regiment was with other wounded British officers on the train from Cologne to Torgau. He later wrote:

> We travelled in third class carriages with the usual guard. The under-officer in charge of us tried the usual shouting method at us, but when he found we were all wounded and unable to move about very quickly he changed his manner, and after getting into conversation with him in the train he turned out to be quite a good fellow and looked after us well, and also prevented any Germans coming and looking at us when the train stopped in the stations.
>
> At one station, some German Red Cross nurses were on the platform with food etc. The under-officer called to them to bring some food, and when they came to the carriage and saw we were English they made some remark that we were '*Schweinehunde Englander*' and that they were not going to give us anything. With that the under-officer dashed out of the train, seized one of the women by the arm, and used some abusive language to her and made her bring some food for us, and also send one of the others off for some hot coffee.

Captain T.B. Butt of the KOYLI was wounded in the leg and arrived at the station at Cambrai around 1 pm on 11 September. He was taken to a small shed full of bales of straw and put with

A heavily guarded column of British troops is marched through the ruins of a Belgian town. As they are wearing field service caps rather than steel helmets, this was probably taken early in the war.

40 English and 100 French soldiers. Towards the end of the afternoon it began to rain, so the guards ordered them out of their shelter and made them stand on the platform for two hours, becoming thoroughly soaked. Two hours later, once the rain had stopped, they were put back in the shed again.

Around 7 pm the train finally arrived and Butt, together with a Lieutenant Backhouse, was put in a cattle truck with nine wounded German privates. One end of the cattle truck was 6in deep in horse dung and they were deposited there for the three-day journey to the camp at Minden. They found their wounded adversaries to be sympathetic to their condition and when meals were brought to the Germans during the trip, they always said that there were eleven of them, not nine and the two extra meals were given to the British. At one station, however, the man put his head into the truck and saw the two Englishmen and at once said: '*Nein, nein. Englander Schweinehunde.*' However, two of the Germans ate their meals quickly and asked for more, which they then passed on to the two officers.

Things turned ugly when a troop train stopped nearby. Butt later reported:

The soldiers all crowded round to hear the battle news and to see the prisoners. One of these men began talking to me in English, telling me what fools we were and how soon we were going to be beaten, etc. He then gave me a peremptory order to come and show myself; this I declined to do, at the same time pointing to my leg. He then pushed another soldier into the carriage, who rushed at me, beating me over the head and generally abusing me. Whilst I was trying to keep him off by holding his throat another man threw a large piece of wood, which hit me on the back of the head. Fortunately our train moved on and these men had to leave the carriage.

To give them their due, the nine Germans in my carriage, who witnessed this, appeared to be very angry about it, but could do nothing. There being no latrine in cattle trucks, the question of performing these duties of nature became most pressing. When the train stopped the French prisoners used to swarm out of their carriages in answer to nature's call; when an Englishman did likewise they allowed him out for about 45 seconds, and would then approach him, bayonet at the ready, shouting '*Einsteigen*' which we soon discovered meant 'Get into the carriage or you will be pricked.'

A German soldier lights a cigarette for a wounded British prisoner at a field dressing station.

Chapter 3

The Camps

The 'official' view of the German attempt to house the vast numbers of prisoners is reproduced below, from the *1915* book printed by them in Berlin. To be fair, the Germans did not expect to have to house so many prisoners of war and had to put extensive plans in place to house and feed them all:

When, after the first battles of the war, after the fall of Liege, Longwy, Maubeuge, Antwerp, the victorious course of our armies in the West, and after the marvellous battle of Tannenberg in the East, hundreds of thousands of prisoners of war were at first taken to the regular camps, where German troops were kept during times of peace. But these, all available barracks and other public buildings were insufficient to receive the overwhelming numbers of volunteers and men called in for service, and new camps had to be specially prepared for the prisoners of war.

Two photographs from Schneidemuhl show the prisoners arriving from the front. After their heavy fighting, fatigued as they were, often having for days not even received sufficient food from their own Army Boards, the first they received was a warm meal. The prisoners from Novo-Georgievsk, who arrived at the prisoners' camp Stralkowo, were less starved and when their magazines were destroyed, they had provided themselves with clothing, boots and many a rouble note. Another photograph from Hammerstein also show us the prisoners fetching dinner after their arrival. The French civilian prisoners of war were heavily laden with bags and parcels. As it was the rule, they were first concentrated in large camps close to the frontier. After a certain quarantine period they were taken to other camps situated more in the interior of Germany, and even then, they had sometimes to be transported again to other camps, or taken to small workers' encampments. The departure, as shown, for example from Stargard, often proceeded amidst the regret and tears of the prisoners, who had grown accustomed to the camp and now feared that elsewhere they would not have it as good.

The next picture is a birds' eye view of one of the newly constructed camps at Zerbst. Besides the prisoners camp proper a smaller camp had to be erected for the guards. The photograph from Döberitz shows how such a camp appears nearby. From the camp at Gottingen the prisoners have, on one side, a view of the venerable old University town, on the other side of the Bismarck Tower and the spurs of the Hartz mountains. The Ohrdruf camp is situated along the range called the Thuringer Wald. Small elevations in the proximity of the camps are utilized for erecting the guards' house, or, for placing machine guns or small field guns in case a revolt or the like should occur. But it has always proved sufficient to impress the prisoners by alarm exercise that the troops guarding the camp are permanently on the alert, so that no such revolt or rising has been reported. The construction of the prisoners' huts was

A fresh batch of Russian prisoners arriving at Schneidemühl camp from the Eastern Front.

Newly-arrived prisoners at Schneidemühl camp waiting to be fed.

At Stralkowo, newly-arrived Russian prisoners from Novo Georgievsk receiving their rations. According to the German account they had pillaged their own stores for boots and clothing after the battle.

Prisoners at Hammerstein line up to receive their rations from the wooden containers in the foreground.

A 'transport' or detachment of prisoners prepares to leave Stargard camp. There appear to be too many for a local working party, so they may be on their way to another camp.

A plan of the newly-constructed prisoner-of-war camp at Zerbst. A smaller camp was constructed nearby for the guards.

ZERBST
KRIEGSGEFANGENENLAGER
CAMP DES PRISONNIERS DE GUERRE

A view of the two barbed-wire fences surrounding Döberitz camp.

Uniformly-constructed barrack huts at Göttingen. On the one side a view of the old university town; on the other side of the Bismarck Tower and the spurs of the Hartz Mountains.

The Ohrdruf camp situated along the range called the Thüringer Wald (Thuringian Forest).

not carried out after a uniform system. On the contrary, the various commissariats and builders were allowed a free hand to erect the accommodations for housing the prisoners according to the available material and the local conditions, only general principles having to be observed: e.g. a given floor and breathing space per head. Our photograph shows the huts at Tuchel made of corrugated sheet metal, whilst on the right at the rear and on the left also the more generally used wooden huts are seen in course of construction.

In the South of Germany very substantial buildings were constructed, as may be seen by the view from the prisoners' camp at Amberg. The view from Aschaffenburg shows that by the aid of existing groups of trees and handsome buildings and gardens even a quite stylish appearance of the camp could be secured. The huts were also erected right in the woods, as for example in Zossen and both guards and prisoners were more as if at a summer resort. The view from the prisoners' camp at Hameln again shows us how, besides by the beautiful surroundings, the camp could be given a handsome appearance by freshly planted, pretty gardens. The first hut is arranged as a school for the children, as it appeared unnecessarily hard to separate these from their parents, held in protective confinement. The camp at Görlitz further illustrates what gardening, performed by the prisoners in their leisure hours may achieve.

Although, owing to the sudden call for them, the most camp buildings were constructed by German contractors and artisans, many additional buildings, and in some instances, the entire plant of huts could be erected by the prisoners of war themselves, under the supervision of the German guarding troops, expert officers and subalterns.

In some cases, in particular in the South of Germany, it was possible to use already existing buildings for housing the prisoners, and so to afford them a home during captivity

Tuchel II: view from a guard tower over the camp, with huts still being built to the left of the picture. Looking at the number of stove pipes and chimneys on the roofs of the huts, they appear to be well heated and the roof is made from corrugated sheet metal.

Amberg prisoner-of-war camp. None of the huts appear to be heated as there is no sign of stove pipes emerging from the rooftops.

One of the camp thoroughfares at Aschaffenburg.

which is very comfortable and is rendered homelike by an older growth of trees (cfr, the photographs from Eichstatt and Schloss Trausnitz). At the camp near Regensburg, the river Danube has been cleverly utilized as a boundary.

A novel type of prisoners' camp was arranged at Danzig, where Russian barges and British steamers were commandeered, anchored along the banks of the Vistula and equipped for housing some 10,000 prisoners of war. Only the kitchens, water-closets, lavatories and baths etc were constructed on land. Owing to an excellent organisation and discipline it has been possible to secure, within this camp produced at a minimum cost, a satisfactory status both as regards the health and the welfare of the prisoners of war.

Prisoner-of-war hospital at Zossen.

Hameln camp with a school (*schule*) on the left and commander's (*commandantur*) hut on the right.

Gardens being tended by the prisoners at Görlitz camp.

Prisoners building the second hospital hut at Wasbek, under the supervision of German guards and contractors.

Prisoners waiting for the evening ration of soup at Eichstatt.

Schloss Trausnitz: prisoners of war billeted in the castle in the south of Germany.

View of the camp at Regensburg, with one boundary of the camp provided by the river.

In some cases also farms, factories and other edifices could be utilized, being equipped for the purpose by the prisoners of war themselves, and by such means, small camps could be established which allowed of more conveniently occupying the prisoners than it was possible in large camps, where, on the contrary, it was more easy to guard the same.

North end of the camp at Danzig with captured Russian and British barges moored alongside. They were used to house up to 10,000 prisoners with only the need to construct kitchens and latrines on the land.

Officers' camps have, almost exclusively, been established in already existing buildings, such as barracks, castles, sanatoria etc. The photographs from Crefeld, Burg, Heidelberg, Konigstein prove that life in these camps ought to be endurable. At one of the most beautiful places in Germany, at the confluence of the rivers Werra and Fulda, an empty factory building, surrounded by high mountains and fine beech forests has been converted into an officers' camp, and the inmates enjoy the benefits of a health resort; here the Russian, French, British and Belgian officers prisoners of war feel very comfortable, once they have accustomed themselves to captivity. The prisoners' camp Clausthal is most romantically situated in the midst of the fir wood forests of the Hartz mountains.

As the view from the prisoners camp at Gottingen shows, the joint life of the prisoners with the guards has led to a certain degree of camaraderie. The prisoners salute the German officers, standing to attention, and are grateful that they are given, after much trouble, a certain comfort, although a strict discipline has to prevail and all luxury is tabooed. The Russian prisoners are particularly cosy in huts which are constructed in excavations, about two feet deep, as these are cool in summer and warm in winter. They gaily decorate these temporary homes with national paintings and carvings.

The camps are, as a rule, encircled by a barbed wire fence, along which leads the beat of the Landsturm patrol. The picture showing a street in the camp of the guards at the Strakowo camp, erected on formerly Russian soil, proves that the Rhenish and Westphalian Landsturm men have known to create a handsome home, tastefully decorated with flowers and garden beds.

View of the camp buildings at Crefeld, used to house officer prisoners of war.

The officers' camp at Burg.

The official German account of their attempts to house the prisoners of war sounds very convincing and the prisoners were no doubt willing to pose for the accompanying photographs if the right persuasion was used. However, the reality was often quite different as the following accounts will show.

Corporal John Brady of the KOYLI fell into the bag on 26 August 1914 at Le Cateau. The stand taken by II Corps temporarily stemmed the German advance and bought valuable

The officers' camp at Heidelberg.

time for the allied forces in the northern sector as they retreated towards the River Marne. However, more than 7,000 British and French soldiers were killed, wounded or taken prisoner, while the Germans suffered approximately 5,000 casualties.

Although Brady's wounds were attended to after capture, he was not given any food or water for the two days it took to travel to Sennelager. Under the jurisdiction of the 7th Army Corps, Sennelager was a large camp near Paderborn in Westphalia, 50 miles south-west of Hannover, situated on open sandy country of heather, pine and bog land. It was used as a summer training camp for soldiers and was still in use for the same purpose by the British Army of the Rhine sixty years later. The camp was divided into four portions, with one of them used for a time to hold captured English fishermen. The first prisoners to arrive had to sleep in the open for a week, until tents were erected and they were each given some straw and a blanket. By this time the men were starving and very weak and lice had begun to appear in their clothing. It was three months before Brady was able to wash his shirt and to wash himself with soap.

The men were forced to work for their captors through the winter of 1914, until they were finally moved into wooden huts,

Prisoners on their way to dinner at the fortress at Königstein.

The officers' camp at Clausthal in the Hartz Mountains.

A photo taken on a Sunday afternoon in Göttingen camp, with two German officers in the foreground.

but without beds, in January 1915. The food given to the men was inadequate, but the first food parcels had begun to arrive just before Christmas. Thereafter it was downhill for Brady as he was sent away with two dozen others to work in a stone quarry. Their food parcels were delayed due to the move and their letters home were being censored and destroyed if they mentioned the true conditions under which they were working.

At the end of July Brady and his men refused to go to work due to the poor conditions. That night they were called out on parade and a German officer appeared with fifteen soldiers who proceeded to fix bayonets. Once again they were told to go to work and once again they

Tuchel, a prison hut dug into the ground and decorated by its Russian occupants. Excavated to a depth of around 2ft, they were supposedly cool in summer and warm in winter.

Russian prisoners used in the construction of barbed-wire fences at Bütow.

refused. Finally they were all escorted to the railway station and taken back to Sennelager where fourteen days in the cells awaited them.

Their trial began at the end of August and an English-speaking officer was sent from Berlin to represent them. They were found guilty of mutiny and sentenced to six months' hard labour;

A street in the Landsturm end of the camp at Stralkowo in Russia.

The entrance to the prisoner-of-war camp at Crossen.

a relief for Brady as he expected to be shot. A month in a civil prison followed, where Brady was employed sawing timber, and then he and his comrades were sent to Cologne where the work was hard and food parcels rare. By February 1916 one of his fellow prisoners had died and another was taken away to hospital, never to return.

Brady was sent back to Sennelager again and thence to Paderborn where he was used for street-sweeping and where he was bashed daily by his revolver-waving guard. As the months went by Brady was sent out on a number of working parties, or *arbeits kommandos* as the

In the early days at Münster Lager, men were forced to sleep in tents until huts could be constructed.

Germans called them. Brady often refused to work, spending time in a number of jails instead, surviving on bread and water. Eventually Brady and one of his comrades found themselves at Langricht, about 80 miles from Minden, in the company of around sixty French prisoners. Their work was to produce wire and since it could be used for the enemy war effort, they once again refused to work. A severe beating and another week in jail followed, but by now the Germans were running out of patience.

Brady and his comrade were sent to work at a mine with 1,400 Russians and 700 Frenchmen. His comrade was sent down the pit and Brady, claiming to be a blacksmith, was given a job in one of the workshops. One month later Brady struck one of the German civilians in the workshop and when he returned to camp he was beaten black and blue by the sentries. He was given fourteen days in the cells on bread and water, but when his time was up he refused to go out to work again and received another beating. The next twenty-eight days were spent in solitary confinement and Brady suffered badly during that period. With only his thoughts for company Brady came to the conclusion that there could be only one ending to his situation: he would escape.

Schneidemühl

In November 1914, while John Brady and his fellow prisoners were still living in tents at the cold and barren Sennelager camp, Private Green arrived at Schneidemühl, near Posen. Schneidemühl was an important railway junction and the camp was located 3 miles out of town on higher ground. Built on sandy ground and surrounded by woods, the camp had a capacity of 40,000 to 50,000 prisoners, although many were away from the camp on working parties.

When Green arrived at the camp it was a bitterly cold morning and the men were shivering in their khaki uniforms, their greatcoats having been taken from them by their captors. After three hours standing in the cold, they were taken fifty men at a time for inoculations. They did not know what the injections were for and took a dim view of the same needle being used for all. Then they were issued with blankets, spoons and basins and marched to the cookhouse, where they were given 'pig's meal' and potatoes. Although they were very hungry, very few ate the concoction. Their prison cells for the time being would be in dugouts: holes in the ground covered with straw.

Their first full day in Schneidemühl would provide them with an example of the brutality that could be expected from their captors. They began queuing before dawn for their breakfast of bread and coffee. In the ensuing crush and scramble with the Russian prisoners, a Private Bowlam of the Coldstream Guards was struck by a sentry. He grabbed hold of the sentry's bayonet and struggled with him before breaking away and escaping. He was eventually caught and beaten by the guards on the orders of the officer in command, but died from his injuries.

The prisoners' routine was scheduled around mealtimes, if indeed they could be called that. Their breakfast consisted of coffee and black bread at 6 am, followed by so-called soup at 11.30 am and coffee again at 5 pm. Raw herring was given in place of meat twice a week, but the prisoners usually sold them for around five pfennigs for cigarettes or bread.

After ten days living in the dugouts, the prisoners were moved into barracks, each block comprising two rooms with around sixty men in each. The majority of the prisoners were Russian, but half a dozen English were put in each room with them. This was very unfortunate as most of the Russians were infested with lice and typhus fever soon broke out in the rooms. In the middle of December the English prisoners were moved from Number 1 Lager to Number 2, but within three months all but eleven of them had been or were in the camp hospital fighting for their lives. Twenty of them would die before the outbreak was under control. The death toll for the Russian prisoners was around thirty men per day and 11,000 would perish in eight months.

As if the typhus outbreak was not enough, the men also had problems caused by their own leaders. Private Green later reported:

Another detriment to our being ill, was that we were compelled to walk round every day for two hours – ten to 11 and three to four. In rain, frost, snow and without

British prisoners of war arriving at their new camp. They appear to have managed to keep hold of their greatcoats and other possessions.

British prisoners receiving their rations at Cottbus camp.

any trousers at times, when they were being fumigated. On 15th January I fainted twice from weakness before seeing the doctor. I came out of hospital on 28th January in a very groggy state. Myself, Jackson from the Coldstream Guards and Corporal Hill from the Gloucester Regiment came out together. We were the first to go into the dugouts from hospital. Jackson soon again went back and died there.

In May, Lawson from the Scots Guards and Barnsley from the Coldstreams were awarded 28 days in the cells for insubordination to Drill Sergeant Hogan who was in charge of us. This was caused by an officer coming and seeing the men in the room, not walking around as they should have been. Their cell diet consisted of two days bread and water, one day soup. I am not far wrong in saying all our troubles were caused by our head NCO – Hogan. He was a rotter and would fare bad if matters were properly investigated on our return home. Many a word said or something done has he reported – to keep in with the enemy.

On one of the last days of August the men underwent a strict medical inspection and the fittest were told that they were going to work in the mines. Green was one of those chosen and he joined his comrades for a thirty-six-hour journey in cattle trucks to a place named Bursigwerk in Oberschlesien. An hour's march from the station took them to Schlafhaus II in Kronprinzenstrasse where they were to live. The work in the Preussen Grube was hard, with ten-hour shifts mostly at night, with little respite at the weekends. One young lad by the name of Davis spent three weeks in Beuthen hospital and then went back again a few days after his release. He died on New Year's Day 1916.

Green later wrote:

22nd March 1916. We were very lucky this day, finishing work at 2 pm. The other shift had only been working two and a half hours when a terrible explosion occurred in the Pockhammer district. I had been working in the same place for a fortnight. Fourteen Germans and eight Russians lost their lives. All available men with safety lamps were set to work, finding bodies.

In the last week of May a Welsh newspaper found its way into the camp and the news was not good. It revealed the surrender of British forces at Kut-al-Amara in Iraq with 2,000 English and 6,000 Indian troops being taken prisoner with another 1,000 left behind ill or wounded. On 2 June a telegram arrived at the mine announcing the results of a naval engagement at sea. Known later as the Battle of Jutland, the German navy had lost seven ships and the English eleven and the Germans were claiming victory.

On 6 June, the local German newspaper announced the death of Lord Kitchener, who was on board HMS *Hampshire* when she was hit by a mine or torpedo off the Orkney Islands. More than 600 men were lost including Kitchener and two dozen of his staff officers.

Around October 1916 the prisoners began to realize that things were not going smoothly for the German Empire. They were paid three German marks per week for their work in the mines but on Monday, 2 October they were given only two and some only one and a half marks. The remainder had been stopped because the German Reichstag had asked the people for another war loan. The *Beuthener Zeitung* newspaper published a list of the mines with the amount given voluntarily by war prisoners!

Surrender at Kut

The German newspapers did not need to exaggerate the size of the British defeat at Kut-al-Amara. The Mesopotamian campaign was not going well. The advance on Baghdad had failed and the BEF was surrounded by the Turks at Kut. On 29 April 1916, after living on starvation rations for weeks, five generals, 400 British officers, 2,700 British soldiers and 9,000 Indian officers and soldiers surrendered after a siege lasting 147 days. While the officers were transported by boat or train, the other ranks had to march the 100 miles north to Baghdad and 200 miles thereafter. In their weakened condition hundreds fell by the wayside en route to the Turkish prison camps. The treatment in the camps was very poor and by the end of the war 4,250 of 11,800 men who had left Kut on 6 May 1916 were dead.

One of the British officers, Brigadier Kenneth B.S. Crawford of the Royal Engineers, later wrote in his diary:

Things were going badly with us inside the Kut perimeter. We were assailed chiefly by various intestinal diseases resembling cholera, and were burying from 30 to 50 men a day, latterly as many as 80 in a day. Efforts to send us food by air failed owing to the shortage of aircraft, and enemy interference. It took a fortnight to send us one day's ration. From 24 January 1916 we had been on three quarters rations and the meat issued was either horse or mule. For some time after that the Indian troops refused to eat this meat. The ration was gradually reduced, and by 9 April we were down to 5 ounces of bread, and by 17 April to 4 ounces, with a similar quantity of meat. By this time nearly all the Indians were eating the meat issued. At least, they agreed to eat the horses – the British had to eat the mules.

By 27 April no food was left, General Townshend began negotiations with Khalil Bey, the Turkish commander, and on the morning of 29 April the Turks were allowed to march into the town. Our force, consisting of 400 British officers, 2,700 British soldiers, and about 9,000 Indian officers and men, was taken prisoner. After the officers and other ranks had been separated into different groups, they were marched off to the Turkish camp

British and Indian prisoners taken at the fall of Kut.

7 miles up the river. I was amongst the wounded, who with the sick remained in Kut for another fortnight.

At the beginning of our captivity the words with which we were greeted by almost every Turkish officer we met were: 'You are our honoured guests!' In view of the rough time we had during our journey up into Asia Minor, which took four months in my own case, and in view of the number of deaths that occurred, these words became a standing joke amongst the prisoners and were always brought up at our various dinners and meetings after the war.

Townshend's second-in-command General Mellis did take up very strongly with the Turks the bad treatment of the other ranks and secured some improvements – but the improvements came rather late and the Turks soon got tired of Mellis, and sent him off by himself in a carriage by the Euphrates route so that he saw no more of the prisoners.

As soon as the prisoners arrived in the Turkish camp near Kut, they were handed out the Turkish ration of small round loaves of black bread. These loaves were about the size and shape of a large thick biscuit; 5 of them made up the full bread ration. In the field, the Turks baked their bread away back at the base and sent it up to the front in sacks, usually weeks old, and it was so hard that it had to be soaked before one could eat it. We didn't know this and in any case it was pretty poor sort of fare for stomachs that were mostly in bad order. Of the prisoners who entered the Turkish camp that morning nominally fit – that is not on the sick list – 91 were dead the same night. It is necessary to be very, very careful when making a complete change of diet like that, unless one is in perfect trim.

The Turks made a very great difference between their treatment of officers and their treatment of other ranks. The officers travelled up to Baghdad in barges, and were allowed a suitcase and a roll of bedding each. But the men had to march, as there was no railway. They could take with them only what they could carry. Beyond Baghdad there was a 17 mile length of railway which took them on to Samarra; but after that all ranks had to march about 200 miles across the desert in the middle of the hot weather before reaching the railway on the far side.

Officers on the march were allowed a pack animal between two to carry their baggage, but the other ranks had to carry their kits, and were flogged along with whips by the Arab guards if they fell behind at all. Hundreds of them couldn't keep up, and died of cholera or dysentery by the way. In two places there were long marches of 30 miles or more without intermediate watering places. So many men died on these marches that the later parties coming after them were taken round another way, so that they shouldn't see the bones of their comrades by the roadside.

There was a Gurkha battalion in Kut (the 2/7). These little men accomplished the whole distance marching as a battalion in formation under their Gurkha officers; which was a very fine performance in the circumstances, and a great help to the weaker men amongst them. It was most inspiring to see such a good regimental spirit.

The sick and wounded travelled by water from Kut to Baghdad, a distance of 200 odd miles as the river goes, and arrived there about the middle of May. I was with 3 sick officers – 2 British and 1 Indian – almost the last party to go through, and a very small one. From Baghdad we went on much as the others had done before us. Sick and wounded officers were supposed to have animals to ride, but they usually joined us onto convoys of sick soldiers and we had to give up our riding animals to men who were very badly in need. We had one long march of 32 miles, which we had to do without refilling our water bottles. It was hot weather and we usually marched about four hours in the morning and four in the evening. When we came to Mosul we had 5 days' rest.

Eventually we reached the far railhead at Ras al-Ayn, and travelled the rest of the way in third class railway carriages, except when passing the two mountain ranges – the Taurus and the anti-Taurus – one of which we crossed in carts and the other in German lorries. The Germans were driving railway tunnels through those two ranges. As unskilled labour they took British prisoners for one tunnel, and Gurkhas for the other. I reached my prison camp at Afion on 27 August 1916 – four months after the fall of Kut – and found myself along with 50 British and Australian officers captured at the Dardanelles (including 10 naval officers). There were also 80 Russians and a dozen Frenchmen.

The accommodation was adequate – each officer got about the same space as Generals and Brigadiers got at Shirakawa – but in addition each mess of 10 officers had a dining room, a kitchen, a store and a closet. Almost the whole of Asia Minor is at least 3,000 feet above sea level and the mountains go up to 10,000 feet. Afion is in the centre, about 120 miles south-west of Angora. The summers are warmer than in England, and the winters are much colder. We were usually allowed out of our camps three times a week for a couple of hours with a sentry, to go shopping or walking, and were allowed 3 British orderlies for every 10 officers. Officers received pay at five shillings a day, and bought their own food. They received no rations.

Other ranks received a ration of bread, meat-soup, salt, sugar, coffee and tobacco; but drew no pay, except occasionally a little working pay. The NCOs and men at Afion were housed in the Armenian church, which was a mighty cold place in winter, and they suffered a great deal from influenza, asthma, pneumonia etc. I saw as many as four bodies in a day carried past our houses for burial. Of the British NCOs and soldiers captured in Kut, 4 out of 5 died in captivity – about half the deaths were from intestinal diseases in the hot plains of Iraq, and the remainder mostly from chest troubles during the severe winters in Anatolia.

We could buy Turkish leather shoes (boat-shaped things with no laces), rough Anatolian stockings, cotton stuffs and thick white felt, out of which

British prisoners in the Turkish camp at Kiangheri in Asia Minor.

warm waistcoats could be made. The Ambassador also produced warm clothing, sent by the Red Cross. The Protecting Power was the USA during our first year. After the Americans came into the war, the Dutch Ambassador took over the job. We received most of our letters from home and about half our private parcels; and we wrote a short letter to our people once a month.

I spent a year and 9 months at Afion and then went to another camp between that and Smyrna where I passed the last 5 months of the war. About 60 of the officers at this other place were in a barracks just outside the town, and we were all out of the barracks one night, attending an amateur performance of the musical comedy *Theodore and Co.*, when a fire started in the middle of the town. It was a town of 20,000 inhabitants or so and densely populated. Turkish houses are built in wood frames to allow for earthquakes, the fire-fighting arrangements are primitive and when a town catches fire it is extraordinarily hard to put it out. By next morning this town had been almost entirely burnt to the ground. 35 officers (including myself), who lived in houses in the town, lost everything. I was left with what I stood up in – a cotton suit, SCWB warm overcoat, Turkish shoes, two small drinking glasses and an empty brandy bottle.

Towards the end of our captivity conditions eased up a good deal, and we were allowed to roam about within certain limits without a guard. The fire took place on 28 September 1918, and we were on the way to a new camp when the Armistice with Turkey was declared on 1 November. We were diverted without delay to Smyrna, where we waited for British ships to take us home. I sailed from Smyrna with a shipload of other prisoners on 18 November; and after a fortnight in Egypt and 7 days in a train crossing France, I reached my home a week before Christmas.

Sunk at Jutland

The Battle of Jutland was fought from 31 May to 1 June 1916 in the North Sea, near the coast of Denmark's Jutland peninsula. It was the largest naval battle of the war and the only full-scale clash of battleships. The Royal Navy's Grand Fleet under Admiral Sir John Jellicoe engaged the Imperial German Navy's High Seas Fleet, with 151 British ships facing 99 German vessels. By the time the smoke had cleared, both sides were claiming victory. The Germans lost 11 ships and 2,500 killed, but 14 British ships were sunk and over 6,000 crewmen killed. Another 177 British sailors were captured, including Seaman Byrne who later wrote:

> The enemy kept up his murderous fire on our helpless little ship, until she began to sink. The final order of 'every man for himself' came none too soon, as we had just time to launch the boats, after which I jumped into the water, and was picked up by our little boat twenty-five minutes later. In the meantime our ship had sunk stern first, with the white ensign still flying. She was riddled from bow to stern on the side facing the enemy and hardly a scar on the other side.
>
> Our fleet was steaming on a similar course to that of the enemy and was soon out of sight, there we were left bailing out our boat with our caps. We had a few wounded with us, and a few in the carley float, we also had a few killed, and I think that we were lucky to be alive after the broadsides the enemy had put into our ship. We had been paddling about, watching hopelessly the enemy ships passing by about four miles away, there seemed to be hundreds of them, and the last but one in their line turned and steamed towards us and took us on board.
>
> They were good to us and gave us some black bread, coffee and fish and we were refreshed. As time went on the ship steamed up and joined the others, it was dark by now and the sea was getting very rough, the German sailor bade us sleep, but that was out of the question as we were still thinking about those who had gone down in our ship. During the night the British were chasing the Germans, and we had many scares, it was lucky for us that we were in a fast ship and managed to avoid action with the British. If the ship that we were held prisoners in had been sunk, we would have gone down with it like rats in a trap, because the sentry had been ordered to keep us below until we arrived in harbour the next morning.

Byrne and his shipmates were taken ashore in Wilhelmshaven and marched through the streets where the civilian population put their hands across their throats and called them swines. All except the wounded were sent to Dulmen camp and then on to Brandenburg, a town south-west of Berlin used to hold naval and mercantile marine prisoners. Upon arrival they were inoculated four times in the chest for different diseases. The camp was in an abandoned terracotta factory and they were overcrowded there and the food was mainly potato soup, parsnips and horse meat.

Life in the camp was very hard and when volunteers were asked for, Byrne and fourteen of his comrades stepped forward and were taken to a farm. Fifteen others were told that they were going to work at a farm but found themselves at a munitions factory instead. They rightly refused to carry out any war-related work and were starved for the next two days as a result. Finally they were sent elsewhere to work.

Byrne and his comrades were billeted in a loft over a cow and sheep shed, their bedding just straw and a blanket. Their sleep would be disturbed by fleas, mice and the sound of the animals below them. The farmer paid them three pence per day and promised them a raise of a penny a day, but when the extra money failed to appear they went on strike and refused to leave the loft. Their strike was brought to a swift end twenty-four hours later, with the arrival of half a dozen Prussian troops who broke the door down and forced them out at bayonet point.

Two months later Byrne and his comrades were sent to a factory to carry out non–war-related work. They found French and Russian prisoners already there and were informed that over 1 million French and 3 to 4 million Russians had been taken prisoner, along with half a million British. The Russians had no protecting power to look after their interests and were treated worse than dogs; two were shot during the time Byrne was there. He later recalled that half the Russians could not write their own names, most of them being strong peasants. They told him that they had to wait in their trenches for their comrades to be wounded or killed before they could have a rifle or a machine gun.

As winter approached the prisoners began to see civilians in the potato fields as they marched back to camp in the darkness. Although the penalty for potato theft was very heavy, these night–time raids became more frequent as the time came to gather in the crop. Thereafter crowds of hungry civilians arrived to pick up any potatoes missed by the harvesters. It was going to be a long cold, hungry winter, both for prisoners and civilians.

Because of the environment and economic climate in which the average private soldier lived back in England, he was probably no stranger to cold and hunger. However, for the officer class it was a world far removed from the one they were accustomed to at home.

Captain J.A.L. Caunter of the 1st Battalion, Gloucester Regiment was taken prisoner at Gheluvelt on 31 October 1914 and arrived at Crefeld prisoner-of-war camp on 2 November, along with ten other officers brought in from various parts of the Ypres front. A German breakthrough to Ypres was expected during the evening and as the prisoners were taken to the German rear they saw thousands of fresh troops massed behind the lines. The prisoners were aware that all units facing the enemy were fighting hard and that nothing was left in reserve. How could the Germans fail to use this great opportunity?

The treatment of the prisoners taken in 1914 was bad, but varied depending on where and when they were captured and by whom. Saxon troops were considered to be better captors than Prussians. One of the British soldiers captured with Caunter was made to carry a heavy German pack that bumped up and down on his open wound. When the prisoners asked for water at the Aix-la-Chapelle railway station, the Red Cross 'ladies' replied: 'For an Englander? *Nein*!' At Cologne station German officials hauled three or four British privates out of the cattle trucks and placed them on the platform to be baited by the populace, largely comprising women.

The barracks of the Crefeld hussars, now surrounded by barbed wire, were large and strongly built. The prisoners occupied three large buildings and a fourth smaller one provided mess rooms and canteen. There was a gravel parade square in the middle of the ground between the buildings and this was used for exercise. It was about 140 yards long and 80 yards wide. It would be used as a football ground by the officers and in the summer it was turned into tennis courts.

The commander of the region that included Crefeld was General Von Bissing, the man responsible for the death of nurse Edith Cavell when he assumed command of Belgium. An order signed by the general was posted on the walls of the camp, informing all the prisoners that they were the inferiors of all Germans, whatever rank they might hold. The order also warned the prisoners against trying to 'evade their fate by escaping'. It continued: 'The guards are earnest men, knowing their duty.' This caused the nickname 'earnest men' to be given to them.

For the first year of captivity seven officers would be allocated to the smaller rooms and fourteen to the larger ones. At first they had a cupboard each, but as the rooms filled up over time seven officers had to use four cupboards between them. The beds were iron frames with wooden planks supporting a hard mattress, filled with either straw or wood shavings. During the first few months they only had one small oil lamp between seven officers, so it was impossible for everyone to read at the same time.

Nearly all the officers' greatcoats and waterproofs had been taken away from them at the time of capture, so when they lined up outside at 8 am and 9.30 pm for roll-call they draped their blankets over their shoulders and shivered in the cold. A supply of soldiers' greatcoats would be sent to them through the American Embassy at Christmas.

During the first winter there were about 250 Russians, 200 French, 120 English and a few Belgian officers in the camp. Food parcels began arriving in December but the Germans made the officers pay duty on them for a time; an annoyance in the beginning as they did not have much money with them. Eventually arrangements were made for officers to cash cheques through Cox in London.

As time went by, conditions in the camp improved but until the summer of 1915 they had great difficulty in getting permission to do anything to make themselves more comfortable. In the early summer of 1915, thirty-five British officers were sent to Cologne to be imprisoned in cells as a reprisal against the alleged maltreatment of German submarine crews. As the weather improved in June, three Russian officers made a successful escape from the camp. Three more escaped the following night but were recaptured. They had managed to cross the Dutch frontier 18 miles away, but got stuck in the swampy ground and had to re-cross the frontier into Germany in search of a way round. However, they were seen by a German patrol and recaptured.

The whole affair was badly managed. It was accepted that each party of escapers be given at least twenty-four hours start, so that they might have a chance of getting across the frontier 18 miles away. It was essential to prevent the Germans discovering their disappearance at roll-calls. If anyone was missed, the frontier guards would be warned by telephone to be extra vigilant.

Elsewhere in Europe, the Austro-Hungarian Empire was establishing the first concentration camps for Serbian prisoners. At the end of December 1915 the first truck rumbled through the gates of the new camp at Doboj, Bosnia and Herzegovina, where more than 45,000 Serbs would be detained in inhumane conditions.

A total of 45,791 people would be held here: 16,673 men, 16,996 women and children and 12,122 Serbian soldiers and the elderly from Herzegovina, Sarajevo and Romania and border areas of Serbia and Montenegro and Bosnia and Herzegovina. Some 12,000 of them did not survive.

Chapter 4

All the Comforts of Home

According to the Germans, everything was being done to make the prisoners' stay as comfortable as possible. Their book *1915* stated:

Several of our illustrations show interior views of the huts in a prisoners' camp. Of course, each prisoner cannot be provided with a spring-mattress bed. He must be satisfied with a plank bed; but he always has a straw filled mattress, pillow and two or three blankets; most beds are, besides, separate from each other. There is always a certain, so-called day room, where the meals are taken and the prisoners spend the day, while indoors, and in which boxes, cases and cupboards are provided for them to keep their small belongings. The walls of these rooms are sometimes, as shown in the photograph from the Erlangen camp, artistically decorated by the prisoners themselves.

The officer prisoners of war are always housed in rooms, and generals and staff officers are given, as far as possible, each a separate room, while the other officers must be satisfied with one room for every two or more at a time.

Prisoners eating their meals in what appears to be a 'day room' in Minden I.

A sleeping dormitory in Norderstapel. No separate beds are provided and the straw-filled mattresses and pillows are laid on the floor.

The wall of a French prisoners' hut in Erlangen.

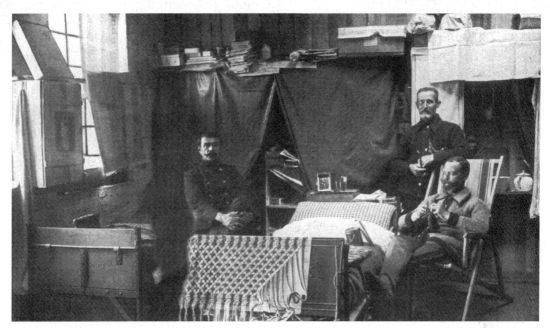

Two officers share a room in the camp at Halle.

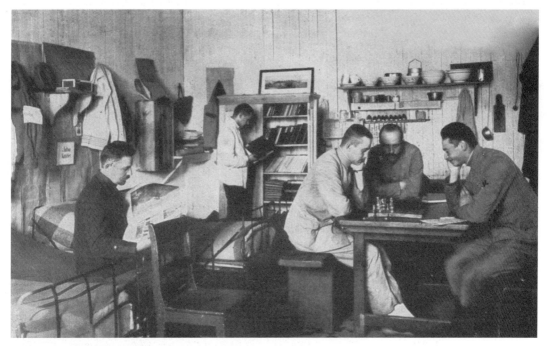

Officers playing chess in their room at Stargard.

After the huts for housing the men were completed, the next task was to provide practicable roads. In many camps an extensive use has been made of field railways, on which coal, provisions and building material are conveyed from the trunk line to the camp, and the products or waste taken from the camp.

The camp railway at Güstrow, used to bring supplies and building materials to the camp.

The boiler house in Salzwedel, used for providing hot water for kitchens, disinfection plants and baths.

The prisoners' canteen in the Russian camp at Gross Poritsch. It is difficult to make out what they are selling but note the absence of any items on the tables.

The prisoners' canteen at Celle. Items here were often scarce and overpriced.

Milk for sale in the canteen at Cassel.

A booth at Cassel selling provisions to any lucky prisoner who had money to spare or something of value to trade.

The camps are also provided with extensive power plants for electric lighting, pumping water and for the generation of steam for kitchens, disinfection plants and the baths.

Particular care is devoted to the arrangement of the kitchens, baths and closets; water service and canalisation had to be provided everywhere. Furthermore canteens have been arranged, be it that there is a single selling booth for the whole camp, or that several small booths are erected for the various sub-sections of the camp, in which, with the assistance

Fire engine practice at the camp at Erfurt.

Fire-fighting practice at Regensburg camp.

of the prisoners, various kinds of food, polishing materials, sewing materials, tobacco, non-alcoholic drinks and other small utensils are sold.

As the huts are generally constructed of wood and there is a constant great danger of fire, fire extinguishing provisions had to be made everywhere. Under the superintendence

Civilian prisoners in the camp at Traunstein practise their fire-fighting and evacuation procedures.

At Aschaffenburg camp Russian prisoners are attempting to rear rabbits, although none appear to be visible in this picture.

of their German guards or instructors the prisoners willingly submitted to the respective drill. Our photographs show Russian and French prisoners at fire-brigade drill.

But also in small details the camps have been improved and developed as far as possible; and the prisoners have been induced to rear rabbits, fowl and even pigs for utilizing the camp waste.

Feeding the Prisoners:

4,500 boilers, each of a capacity of 500 litres or 100 gallons are required for preparing one single meal for 1.5 million heads. This fact alone shows the enormousness of the task of feeding the prisoners of war. If 100 grammes of one single material is to be dispensed to each prisoner, this will mean for the whole lot 3,000 hundred weight. Potatoes, the most important item in the feeding of the prisoners, are allowed at the rate of 1,000 grammes per head and day, thus making a total of 30,000 hundred weight. In order to cover the requirement in meat for all prisoners of war 600 head of cattle must be killed each day.

At first the feeding of the numerous prisoners of war had to be accomplished as well as it was possible for the time being, but gradually special arrangements could be made in this direction.

First of all the principle of individual management was adopted, ie the respective camp commandants themselves managed the feeding of the inmates, as the method of contracting had, in many instances, not proved satisfactory. The feeding was placed on a scientific basis, in so far as fixed allowances were made per head and day, viz

Initially 85 grammes, later 90 grammes albumen
Initially 40 grammes, later 30 grammes fat
Initially 475 grammes, later 500 grammes hydrocarbons.

With an extra allowance of ten percent for prisoners doing very hard work or having been underfed. For each camp, feeding schedules had to be prepared, similar to those shown below. This obliged the controlling officers to constant consideration and calculation. This system, besides, affords a reliable guarantee that each prisoner receives sufficient food, and, on the other hand, it prevents all waste, a fact of the utmost importance for the feeding of the population of the country. The more important provisions and preserves are purchased in bulk by the Ministry for War and distributed upon demand to the various prisoners' camps. It has been found that the wholesale prices were 15%, the retail prices even 50% higher than the prices thus paid, so that by such methods many millions were saved for the Treasury.

The provisions are taken to the camps by rail or trucks as shown in our illustrations. Potatoes and vegetables are cleaned in separate sheds and then cooked in the boilers together with meat, flour, legumes and other ingredients. In some of the prisoners' camps there exist central kitchens, even such with the latest steam cooking ranges, but the most still employ boilers of, on the average, 100 gallons capacity over direct fires. 10,000 men may be easily fed from one kitchen and this affords the advantage of wholesale work and a better supervision, whereas when several small kitchens are employed, each for not less than 1,000 men, the distribution of the meals is the more easy. Our illustration shows such a kitchen, in which rows of 10-30 boilers are arranged, which are fired and filled from one side, and discharged from the other side, prisoners of war performing all manipulations under the supervision of German guards. In hospitals and officers' camps the kitchens have a better equipment, as may be seen from the next picture. Even the officer prisoners of war have undertaken to manage with the aid of their orderlies, their own kitchens, although it frequently caused much difficulty to meet the tastes of the various nationalities assembled. A trustee of the prisoners must always be present in the kitchen and express any wishes of theirs. Of course, kitchen utensils of all kinds are provided, and the bill of fare is posted up publicly in the kitchen, as may be seen on the photograph from the camp at Minden.

As a rule, the prisoners welcome being detached to kitchen duty. In a camp containing 10,000 prisoners, in which two hundred weight of potatoes are dispensed daily, at least 100 men or more have to be occupied with the peeling of the potatoes. But when more important work was found for the prisoners of war, peeling machines had to be resorted to and were employed in a number of camps.

In many camps also a camp bakery has been established, frequently with the latest types of steam ovens, or with brick ovens built by the prisoners themselves, and as there are always professional bakers amongst them, the baking of fresh bread in the camps has proved very successful. Also the slaughtering of cattle and pigs in the camp has proved satisfactory, and

The provisions store at Güstrow camp. Potatoes and other vegetables would be cleaned in separate sheds and then cooked in boilers with meat, flour, legumes and other ingredients.

At Grafenwöhr camp, the 'buying department of the prisoners' canteens'.

Washing day at Friedrichsfeld camp.

Schneidemühl camp prisoners cooking dinner in large boilers under the supervision of their guards.

The camp kitchen at Gütersloh with the large boilers in the background and the smaller containers that would be used to deliver the food to the prisoners.

Hann-Munden, the kitchen in the officers' camp [Hann = Hannover?].

professional butchers amongst the prisoners delight in preparing the meat of the slaughtered beasts, and in making enormous quantities of fresh sausage. The bones are boiled down in steam boilers to a savoury beef-soup.

In the camps of ordinary prisoners, frequently coffee with sugar is given as first meal, mostly, however, a warm soup or gruel. The 300 grammes of bread, which each prisoner receives per

The menu board in the Minden II camp kitchen.

Peeling potatoes in the courtyard of the hospital in Friedrichsfeld. In a camp of 10,000 men, 200 cwt of potatoes would have needed to be peeled daily.

day, are generally consumed at the first or second meal. At noon, the prisoners receive the principal meal of the day, consisting of potatoes, vegetables and meat.

In workers' camps it will be advisable to make a daily extra allowance of 100 grammes of bread and 10% meat, legumes, fish, fat and oil. The above schedule is particularly suited for Russian prisoners of war. For other nationalities, changes should be made in the dishes and their preparation.

As a rule, the meat is replaced twice a week by fish, of course to a larger quantity. In the evening one litre of good bean soup or potatoes with herrings, or gruel with fruit, potato salad with sausage, tea with bread and cheese or the like more is supplied.

Potato-peeling machines in the kitchen at Wittenberg camp.

The bakery in Gütersloh camp.

The meals are distributed either in large tubs, one for each section of 10 to 50 men, or, the prisoners line up and approach the boilers in single file, holding their dinner bowls in their hands, and receiving their portions of one to one and a half litres. In the civilian internment camps the distributing of the meals is not performed with such military order, but also here care is taken that no one is omitted, and that each inmate receives a full and sufficient meal. The French prisoners have in many camps been afforded in form of small cooking ranges, the means for preparing with the food sent to them from home and the food supplied in camp regular several course dinners or suppers according to their own tastes. The Russians, on the other hand, enjoy the permission to prepare their indispensable tea around a wood fire in the camp yard. The meals are eaten in the huts at small or large tables. The officers' camps

A pig about to be butchered in the Danzig-Troyl camp. Professional butchers were often found among the prisoners of war.

Large tubs of food ready for distribution at Wasbek camp. Each prisoner would receive between 1 and 1.5 litres of soup.

frequently have large and lofty dining halls. But whoever, for reasons of his own, be it to be able to take his meals according to his religious rites, be it to enjoy comforts sent from home, desires to dine alone, will find a quiet corner for doing so. In the workers' camp the meals are taken and enjoyed in the open air.

If the ample, yet plain food supplied in camp should not be sufficient for any of the inmates, he is allowed to buy various kinds of additional food in the canteens, paying for these with money either sent from home or earned by himself. Great attention is paid to the dispensing of the bread rations. And lastly provision is made in all camps, that nothing goes to waste; whatever is left over in the form of potato skins and bits of food, is utilized for feeding the pigs kept in camp, which eventually, by the circulation of matter, terminate their existence in the kitchen.

On 4 November 1914 Mr Edward Page Gaston visited Döberitz prisoner-of-war camp, on behalf of the US Ambassador in Berlin. He delivered supplies including 800 pairs of drawers, 1,200 undervests, 1,700 pairs of gloves and 600 greatcoats, the latter having been lost or stolen on capture. A further 1,900 greatcoats and 1,000 pairs of boots were requested.

The distribution of the supplies was watched with envy by the French, Belgian, Russian and Serbian prisoners in the camp. So far their governments had made no effort to assist them and as far as the Russians and Serbs were concerned, help would be a long time coming. At that time the prisoners were not separated into nationalities. As far as the Germans were concerned, allies who fought together could be put in the same barracks together. This caused a number of problems, especially between the British prisoners who preferred windows to be left open to circulate fresh air, while the Russians preferred them to be firmly shut. In addition, most of the Russian prisoners carried lice on their person and typhus would soon break out, infecting all within reach.

Mr Gaston was refused access to the hospital because, he was informed, there were a number of Russian prisoners suffering from the contagious Egyptian eye disease. He did, however, visit

The delivery of Red Cross parcels to Schneidemühl camp near Posen in eastern Germany.

the new prisoners' quarters that were nearing completion: 100 wooden huts were being built with brick foundations and tar-felted roofs that should be able to accommodate up to 15,000 prisoners. The sides of the huts were double-boarded and apparently wind- and weather-proof. They were single-storey, about 80ft by 40ft with 12ft ceilings.

The huts were 8 to 15 yards apart and clustered in compounds of about twenty huts with a large square in the middle for exercise and parades. To each ten huts there was a cookhouse, with four large boilers where food could be prepared and then carried to each hut in large cans. The whole camp was surrounded with barbed-wire fencing 9ft high with an electrified wire running along the top.

Mr Gaston concluded his report with the comment:

> The camp site is in the middle of open fields, in a high and healthy situation, on sandy soil. The rough work is being done by Russians, British, and other prisoners, but the construction work is done by German workmen. Döberitz camp is probably the best equipped war prisoners' quarters in Germany. The British military prisoners are now given an hour's drill, morning and afternoon, by their own non-commissioned officers.

Representatives of the American Embassy in Berlin also visited the lazarettes and hospitals where prisoners of war were being treated. They visited sixteen of the lazarettes in the 7th and 8th Army Corps areas in January 1917. Nine of them were in Aachen, a very ancient town with a population of 150,000, through which all British prisoners being repatriated to England or neutral Holland would pass. Reserve Lazaretts I and II were in use, as well as Reifmuseum, Maschinebauschule, Mariahilf, Luisen, Marien, Elisabeth and Gernison hospitals. Most were

The prisoner-of-war camp at Giessen.

well-built brick or stone buildings that were used as hospitals before the war. In many of the hospitals German civilians, German soldiers and prisoner-of-war patients were treated and in a few instances prisoners of war and German patients occupied beds in the same room or ward. Without exception there was found to be a sufficient number of windows and proper ventilation. Heat was supplied either by radiators or stoves and in most of the lazarettes it was found to be sufficient even during the bitter winter.

The beds were normally iron cots with springs and hair mattresses. Where there were no springs a thick straw mattress was placed under the iron mattress. The bed linen was, as a rule, clean. The visits were generally not previously announced and the American visitors were usually permitted to talk with the patients on their own.

Private Arthur Dawes, York and Lancaster Regiment was a wounded 22-year-old soldier who was repatriated via Switzerland in 1917 and he gave a reliable, balanced account of his time in Friedrichsfeld camp. He was captured on 8 May 1915 at Ypres after being wounded by a 'shrapnel bullet' through the lungs. His wound was dressed the next day at Roulers and he was put on a train as a serious case, destined for Remscheid Hospital. He had no complaints as the military guard and German Red Cross behaved quite well to him. He joined eighty other British wounded in the hospital and underwent an operation to repair his injury. The medical arrangements were good, the wards were comfortable and the doctors careful in their work. He left the hospital on 5 August 1915 for the prison camp at Friedrichsfeld, 60 miles north of Cologne near Wesel. The camp was built on the north-western edge of the Friedrichsfeld army training ground, mainly by French prisoners directed by employees of the Wesel construction company Ziegler. It could hold 35,000 prisoners and was the centre for a large number of working parties or *arbeits kommandos* in the area. There was an open space in the centre of the camp for football and tennis, also gardens with flower beds between the barracks and large vegetable gardens and a potato field tended by the prisoners.

Dawes reported that:

The lodging places were in wooden huts, about 200 men to a hut. The washing and sanitary arrangements were good as there was a plentiful supply of water. We lay on straw mattresses side by side on the floor. I was made mess orderly of my hut to carry food for the men and was responsible that my section of the hut was kept clean. The food was insufficient but was very poor; the coffee was weak and the soup had very little nourishment in it, scarcely any meat. I fed myself on my own parcels from England.

The canteen when I arrived was good and one could buy coffee, sugar, tinned goods etc. but about March 1916 they stopped selling practically all food stuff. However, my parcels from England arrived in good condition and I received a certain amount of under clothing whilst in camp. Smoking was once stopped for eight days owing to certain men being found drunk, but owing to Regimental Sergeant-Major Cullingham this was reduced to two days. Postal arrangements were good, letters and parcels were received regularly. The parcels were opened in our presence, but we were not allowed to receive spirit, wines etc.

I have no complaints to make of the general treatment of the prisoners or the difference of the treatment of nationalities. There was no epidemic of any sort in the camp and religious services were held every Sunday and once during the week by a British Corporal.

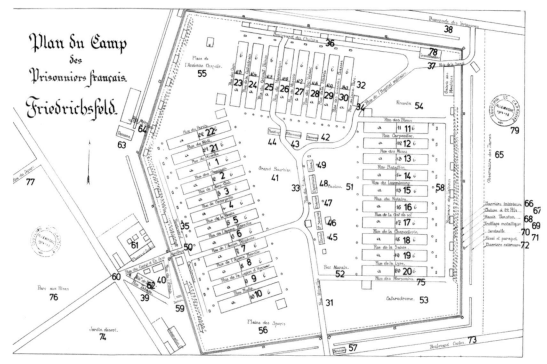

Map of Friedrichsfeld camp.

Corporal Alexander Taylor, 1st Battalion, Scots Guards was also a resident at Friedrichsfeld, having been taken prisoner at Givenchy on 25 January 1915. He had a bullet wound through the right shoulder and one through the right hip and lay on the battlefield for two days until he was discovered. After spending some months in hospital he arrived at Friedrichsfeld in July 1915 to join the 300 other British prisoners among the camp population of some 30,000. He had four hospital stays in sixteen months and found the treatment to be good and the food better than in the main camp. He was given milk and eggs and even lemons for a throat problem. Flushing toilets were even provided in the hospital from the end of 1915.

Conditions improved in the camp with wooden beds replacing the palliasses from March 1916 and covered-in latrines replacing the open-air bucket latrines. Food arrived regularly from England or abroad, except for the bread sent from Switzerland that was usually mouldy when it arrived. The Germans opened all the parcels in the presence of the addressee and all books and letters were taken out of the parcels. Tinned foods were taken and stored, presumably to prevent the prisoners stockpiling them for escape attempts, but they could be drawn when required. One day some photos were discovered in a tin sent in a French parcel, so the whole camp had their parcels stopped for ten days. On another occasion they were stopped for three weeks because a working party refused to go out to work at a mine. The British and French were treated well, but the Russians were treated badly. They did not keep their barracks clean and tidy, and refused to go out on working parties. They were consequently always being paraded and made to stand at attention for two or three hours at a time.

Taylor was eventually passed by the Swiss Medical Commission in November 1916 and repatriated to Switzerland at the end of the year.

Censoring prisoners' mail at Döberitz.

British and French prisoners helping with the distribution of parcels.

Chapter 5

The Jailers

The authors of the book *1915* explained:

In order to maintain the necessary discipline amongst the prisoners, hailing from all enemy countries, all prisoners' camps were placed under military management and superintendence. The war created more important duties for the younger field-worthy troops, and therefore only 'Landsturm' men (the last and oldest reserves) were employed in the camps, and many thousand men, of rank and honour, with house and home, trade and profession to look after, hastened to the hundreds of prisoners' camps to superintend and guard them. Also wounded soldiers, returned incapacitated from the war, took their share. The officers in charge of the camps are former active army officers, who have placed themselves again at the disposal of their country, officers of the reserves, who had resigned and have now again re-entered the service, or others, the health of whom does not permit of their being used for active service. And notwithstanding the fact that these troops are so heterogenous and have, for many years, been out of all military service, an

A group photo of a smart-looking civilian and soldiers from Landsturm Infanterie Ersatz battalions 'Rastatt' and 'Mosbach' taken in 1915, with the commandant seated in the centre at the front. They are guards and administration personnel attached to a Bewachungstruppe des Zivil-Gefangenenlager (Guard troop for civilian prisoners) at the Bureau des Gefangenen, probably at Heidelberg in Baden. Two of them are carrying obsolete 1871 Mauser rifles.

absolutely soldierly life was very soon established everywhere, and the prisoners of war soon recognised that even the oldest Landsturm men were able to fully meet their task.

The same as the arrangement of the camps meant a great deal of work for the Army Board, also the superintending and guarding staffs found serious tasks to be tackled. The surroundings of the camp, the gates and many points within had to be guarded by sentinels, and about one third of the whole staff of guards is employed on such particular service. Besides the prisoners themselves had to be kept under surveillance. For facilitating this, subsections were formed, companies numbering from 200 to 500 men; several such companies form a battalion. Within each company, smaller groups were formed.

On the photograph from prisoners' camp at Guben we see the German guards gathered together to receive the password. Each day numerous items have to be considered and disposed of. When the prisoners arrive from the front, they have first to be examined and their names taken. Curious things have been found in their pockets and bags, such as hall clocks, silver spoons, silk stuffs, ladies' linen and the like more, which, surely, had not been acquired in a lawful manner and therefore were confiscated. Of course also all maps and papers which might be of any importance as regards the military operations, and lastly all arms are taken from them. But all private property is left to them, and only large sums of money are taken in charge, from which the prisoners may draw from time to time, according to requirement.

The same as in their accommodation, there is a great difference in the surveillance of officer and private prisoners of war. The former are kept in separate camps, are treated according to their rank, provide their own food, as they receive pay, and either cater for themselves in cooperation or entrust the catering to a contractor recommended

A section of camp guards wearing a variety of headgear. The warning on the barbed wire informs the prisoners that anyone attempting to climb the wire will be shot.

by the authorities. The troops, on the contrary, are fed and clothed in their camps by the authorities. The daily routine is regulated to the hour and minute. The prisoners are given an opportunity to help in the camp work, and, as far as possible, also to be employed at work outside of the camp. But constant roll calls are necessary, both for ascertaining the number of men and also for selecting any special men needed. Our illustrations show the roll call in Butow and in the civilian internment camp at Rastatt. Each time the prisoners leave camp or return to it, the roll is called and they are carefully counted.

One of our next pictures shows the prisoners being taught, with the aid of an interpreter, the meaning of various signals which call them to the roll call, to fetch dinner and so on.

Roll-call in the Russian camp at Bütow.

At the civilian camp at Rastatt, Number One Company assembles for roll-call.

A Russian working party returns to the camp at Wasbek.

A great deal of work is caused by the censoring of the letters. Each prisoner is allowed to write monthly four postcards and two letters, and may receive an unlimited number of letters and cards. Each letter arriving or leaving has to be carefully examined. It is obvious that a large staff of men is required for this work, and above all linguists. The prisoner of war in Germany has the certainty that every letter will be conscientiously handed to him, provided it does not contain, as it sometimes occurs, false news, which is contrary to the German interests. But even in such cases the addressee is informed that such a letter has arrived.

As the prisoners of war, in particular the French, English and Belgian prisoners, receive very frequent and large remittances, a special money department has been arranged in all large prisoners' camps, by which the moneys are received, changed in the presence of the respective prisoner and paid out to him either all at once or in instalments. Another source of much work is the parcel post service. Parcels arriving are handed over to the prisoners without any restriction, with the exception of false newspaper reports or means to aid them in escaping. 17,000 parcels arrived in one single month at the prisoners' camp Stuttgart II containing 2,400 prisoners. The photographs from the camps Grafenwohr and Landshut show the vans, laden with parcels, as they are fetched daily from the post office. Each parcel has to be opened under the surveillance of a German guard. Surprises are frequent, so for example, a bottle of prohibited alcohol was found baked into a bread, newspapers with caricatures and false reports against Germany are hidden in undervests, and even in soldered preserve tins tools for facilitating an escape have been discovered. Although frequently food sent, arrives in a spoilt conditions, and sometimes the prisoners receive large quantities of delicacies which are not even allowed to their guards, the German Army Board has hitherto not taken any steps to limit this enormous parcel service.

Also comforts sent to them are willingly distributed amongst the prisoners of war. The German officer and subalterns no more regard the prisoners of war as their enemies, but as men entrusted to their care, and are happy when they are able to afford the poor devil, who receives nothing from home, by means of such comforts, some tobacco, tea, chocolate or fresh linen.

Zwickau II distribution of letters to the prisoners.

Censoring prisoners' letters at Parchim. Each prisoner was allowed to write two letters and four postcards each month and could receive an unlimited number of letters and cards.

It is truly no easy task for the aged Landsturm man to perform for so many long months the superintending and guarding service in the prisoners' camps. But in doing so he is upheld and cheered by the idea, that the same as his younger comrades at the front, he is contributing his modest share, with loaded gun and as sentinel, in the service for home and country.

The jailers had *carte blanche* to do whatever they wished with the prisoners. At Friedrichsfeld a party of Russians refused to go out to work and were made to march around the parade ground for two hours at a stretch with filled sandbags. Four men went to hospital after the third day of this treatment. On the fourth day the sandbag parade stopped and they were sent to prison. Another Russian who refused to go out on a working party was put into a wheelbarrow and was beaten and bayoneted. He died in hospital later that day. Two British prisoners tried to escape from a working party sent out from the camp, but they were captured and shot. Their bodies were returned to Friedrichsfeld for burial.

Censoring incoming French mail at Grafenwöhr camp.

Regulations were posted up in every hut, listing the various offences that could lead to punishments: 1) Smoking in rooms; 2) Untidiness of beds and barrack rooms; 3) Untidy outside barracks; 4) Cooking food on stoves (only water was allowed to be boiled on stoves); 5) Being late on parade. Minor offences were punished with three or four days in the cells. Men who refused to go out on working parties got a month's imprisonment in dark cells on bread and water.

Captain W. Gordon Barker, Connaught Rangers, experienced a number of prison camps and their guards and commandants during his time as a prisoner of war. He had been wounded in the thigh at Le Cateau on 26 August 1914 and spent ten days in a French hospital run by the Germans. He was then sent on to Germany with wounded French troops and experienced the usual treatment on

All incoming parcels are vigorously inspected at Königsbrück. Each parcel is opened and examined for prohibited articles, including escape aids.

The arrival of parcels at Grafenwöhr, a luxury not available to Russian or Serbian prisoners.

A delivery of parcels for French prisoners at Landshut.

The parcel store in Friedrichsfeld camp. British and French prisoners could receive parcels from family and friends, regimental associations and the Red Cross.

The German caption to this photo states 'Minden I distributing of presents (comforts)', although there are apparently few presents on view.

An artillery position at Güstrow camp, presumably as a deterrent to unruly prisoners.

A company of Landsturm from Infantry Regiment 102 at Radeburg in 1915.

In this photo, Austro-Hungarian troops punish Russian PoWs at an unidentified PoW internment camp. The manner of the torture exercise is ancient: forcing the victim to suspend all his weight on his distorted arms. After a while, this would become excruciating and even lead to permanent damage.

One punishment meted out to French prisoners was to bind them to a post in all weathers. Bricks would be placed under the prisoner's heels and after he was tied up the bricks would be kicked away so that he was standing on his toes. This unfortunate is being given a drink by a comrade.

the train: lack of food and water, callous guards and irate civilians. At Siegburg he was taken to a Red Cross hospital and well-treated. The next morning he was sent for by the commandant of the fortress, who was very rough and ordered him to be sent to the military prison. He later recalled:

> I was made to walk there uphill, in spite of my wound. I was the only Englishman there and was put in a cell for five days. The place had been an old monastery and the monks were still there. I wrote to the wife of Doctor Korte in Berlin; 'It might interest you to know that I am a prisoner in a common gaol and treated like a criminal.' The Commandant, when he found out that I knew Korte, got rather frightened and the next day I was sent to Ehrenbreitstein military hospital. I was the only Englishman there and I was very well looked after. I had proper diet, and altogether the food was perfectly good.
>
> I was there ten days and then moved on to Wahn. We arrived there after dark, in the pouring rain, and had to walk two miles up to the camp. This was a men's camp. There were four French officers and myself and about 40 French Tommies. In the camp I was told there were 40 British prisoners but did not see them. We were locked up in a tiny guardroom. From there I went in a 4th-class carriage to Halle, taking two days and nights. At one station there was a great deal of noise and we were told the populace wanted to shoot us. One of the guards asked the Red Cross to give us food and they only said; 'No, we do not give anything to Englishmen'. When they offered food to the guard he would not take it unless we were given some, so we were allowed to have some on payment.
>
> Halle was the worst officers' camp in Germany. A filthy, disused factory. There were about 800 altogether, 35 English and the rest Russians, French and a few Belgians. There were 100 in one room, no beds, only dirty palliasses overlapping on the floor. At night it was very stuffy as all the windows were shut. The sanitary arrangements were practically nil. The eating hall was the old foundry of the factory and the food was atrocious. A hot meal was provided in the middle of the day for 50 pfennig and we bought what we wanted for our breakfast and suppers at the canteen. Our mid-day meal consisted of pork or veal and vegetables, very badly cooked.

At the end of September Barker was moved on to Torgau on the River Elbe, where officers were interned in Brückenkopf Barracks and in Fort Zinna:

> There were about 220 English there and we were 10 or 12 in a room. The food was bad and the behaviour of the Commandant Braun was atrocious. Captain Stiven, Royal Scots, died in captivity. He was slightly wounded in the foot and got very depressed and run down. He was sent to the town hospital, where he was locked up alone with a mad French officer for ten days. I saw him the day he left hospital and he seemed very depressed and much worse.

On 28 November, all the English were moved to Burg. They had to walk a mile carrying their things and the wounded were beaten along from behind. Colonel Bond, KOYLI, and Colonel Gordon, VC were both ill-used. When they arrived at the camp the Irish Catholics were separated from the others and given special privileges. Major Haig of the King's Own Scottish Borderers (KOSB) was asked if it was true that the Munster Fusiliers had fired on the KOSB during the retreat from Mons in revenge for the KOSB firing on the Dublin rioters. Barker later recorded that:

The camp (old artillery sheds) was terribly overcrowded, but it was cleaner than Halle. The sanitary arrangements were appalling and the exercise yard quite inadequate. At night there was no ventilation at all. The food was better and we had proper beds and clean sheets. We heard that people were told that the fort of Dixmunden had been captured, and we were the 200 British officers who had been captured there.

At the end of the week Barker was sent back to Halle and it was as bad as before, except that there were only 400 there instead of 800. He was there from December 1914 to June 1915:

We were 30 or 40 men to a room and there were continual arguments with the French about ventilation. A sentry was at each door and the NCOs ran one in for trivial offences. All English parcels were stopped for two months over Christmas and all food taken out and eaten by the orderlies. We were told to give up all gold and they stripped and searched us, bringing in detectives and police dogs. In April Jackson from the American Embassy came to visit us and went round with the officers. The Commandant was a great liar and denied all our accusations.

Captain Priestly came to Halle while I was there the first time. He was looking after some wounded men after the battle of Mons. The orderlies had their clasp knives with marlin spikes. He was called away to attend a case and during that time taken prisoner on the grounds that his orderlies were armed. He was given no trial at all and was put in prison without any definite charge being made. He was in solitary confinement for seven weeks; without books for four weeks and has been very ill since; he nearly went off his head. Captain Davy of the RAMC was taken prisoner by the Germans and they put him and his orderlies in front of them, so that all the orderlies were shot by our own men.

Captain Caunter of the Gloucestershire Regiment (see also Chapter 3, The Camps) was a resident at Crefeld. The town of Crefeld was an important railway centre and the home of 130,000 civilians and the chief velvet and silk factories in Germany. The British officers' camp would eventually be abandoned, leaving just a lazarette for wounded men. It was administered by the 8th Army Corps. Caunter later recalled:

The Commandant, who along with the vast majority of Germans, believed in the inevitable victory over the rest of the world, was a typical autocratic Prussian. He was a petty man, for example, he ordered the cessation of smoking in the camp following the escape of Major Vandeleur in December 1914. The privilege was restored two weeks later, but halted again in the Spring of 1915 after the attempted escape of three French officers. He began to improve in the Summer of 1915 and eventually was considered a fair and just Commandant. He did not get on with the French however and they would turn their backs on him as he came past, in order to avoid having to salute him.

One plucky attempt to escape was made by an officer nick-named 'Peeping Tom'. The refuse heaps and dust bins were cleared out daily by an old German man and a boy, who removed the rubbish in a heavy two-wheeled cart drawn by an old ox. The cart used to leave the camp without being carefully searched and was emptied some distance away. The problem was, how to remain hidden in the stinking rubbish and remain alive at the end of the journey. 'Peeping Tom' borrowed a gas mask from an officer recently brought in from

Canadian prisoners of war in Crefeld in 1917.

the front, put it on and climbed into the cart when the German boy was looking the other way and the old man had departed on some other business. However, he had been spotted by a German who worked in the bath house and who went off to the commandant's office in haste to report the sighting. One of the escaping officer's assistants walked past the cart and warned 'Peeping Tom' that he had been seen and must get out. Suddenly a horrible looking object rose from the middle of the cart, sending a shower of empty tins and other rubbish in all directions. For a moment his peaky masked face peered round, and then leaping from the cart, he went like the wind for the room of a friend in the nearest building. The Germans arrived in force shortly afterwards, but their bird had flown.

One of the German officers was nick-named the Crab, on account of his gait. One day he saw an English officer smoking and took his name, with the result that the victim got three days cells. In the course of his campaign against smoking, he next came up against the French. One of these was observed to be smoking and accused of it. However, he declared his absolute innocence and the Crab was non-plussed. On looking round he found that the whole crowd of Frenchmen were smoking, and roaring with laughter at him. This was too much for him to tackle and he gave it up. Occasionally our allies received him with a chorus of coughs or suppressed cheers if he came on parade late.

A very fine attempt to escape was made by a naval officer, who used the Crab as his model. One evening, knowing that the Crab was busy in the camp and would not be passing out of the Commandantur gate for a few minutes, the Naval officer, dressed a la Crab to the last button, presented himself at the first barrier and got easily through without causing any suspicion. At the next gate however, the sentry, as a matter of form, asked him for his pass, but unfortunately, not being conversant with the language, he was unable to understand what was required of him, otherwise a word in answer and the production of anything at all resembling a pass might easily have sufficed to allay the man's suspicions. Instead of which the sentry had to repeat his question several more times, each time becoming more suspicious of this strangely silent German officer. An arrest quickly followed. The Commandant was extremely amused over the whole affair, and made the naval officer show him how he had copied the Crab walk.

The Commandant then sent for the Crab, who came to his office to find his double staring at him. The Commandant roared with laughter, but the Crab only vouchsafed 'very clever' in English, looking very fed-up all the while.

Things could turn ugly though, as British Private William Lonsdale of the Duke of Wellington's Regiment discovered after he punched a German guard in November 1914. Lonsdale and his 250 fellow captives had failed to assemble quickly enough for the Germans and a general fracas erupted between the prisoners and the guards. Lonsdale was sentenced to death, although, bowing to international pressure, the death sentence was commuted to twenty years in January 1915. He wrote a letter to his wife:

Sorry you heard of my trouble. I did not want you to know of it. I am not allowed to say anything about my case in my letter, so you must wait until you see me again before you can hear my story of the affair.

You can address your letters as usual to Döberitz, as I am in the guard-room here. I am not in prison yet. I expect to remain here till my trial comes to a satisfactory conclusion. When that will be I cannot say, but I am allowed a good lawyer – a German – but he speaks English.

I have left everything to him, and I think he will do his best for me, so I am hoping and trusting that all will end well when the war finishes. I cannot complain of my home or my treatment since I came here on November 10, as everything possible has been done for my comfort and welfare. The men themselves who have to attend to my wants treat me with civility and respect. I am satisfied with everything, and I feel confident what all will come well in the end.

Lonsdale was eventually pardoned by the Kaiser, seizing the propaganda opportunity. It was probably a good thing that Lonsdale was pardoned by the Germans. The Canadians had hinted at reprisals against German prisoners in Canada in return. German prisoners at Fort Henry, Kingston had attacked their guards without provocation in an attempt to escape and the guards had to defend their lives. The *Montreal Star* newspaper suggested that, if Lonsdale was shot, the same fate should befall the German mutineers.

Private Lonsdale who was sentenced to death for striking a guard. He was later pardoned by the Kaiser.

Chapter 6

Sanitary Arrangements and Care of the Sick

From the *1915* book:

A number of prisoners of war, arriving from the East, proved to be infected with cholera, typhus, dysentery and above all the dangerous spotted typhus. This latter disease is particularly feared for reason of its contagiousness and the frequently fatal results to Germans infected with it, whereas the Russians seem to be able to resist its effects to a better degree. As lice were found to be the bearers of the infection, all energy had to be devoted towards dealing with these. Therefore, disinfecting apparatus were provided for every camp, and disinfecting chambers were constructed, in which not only the clothing, but also blankets, straw mattresses etc were freed by steam, hot air or disinfectant vapours, from all parasites and germs of disease. This disinfection is systematically repeated at given intervals, and at the same time the bodies of the prisoners are subjected to a thorough bathing and soaping. The large camps contain for this purpose vast bathing halls. The prisoners of war, who, sometimes for months have not been able to change their clothes rejoice at the benefit

Disinfecting machines used to rid prisoners' clothing of lice in use at Sagan. The camp had a capacity of 6,000 prisoners and was built 5 miles from the town on a flat sandy plain surrounded by forests. In the Second World War it would be known as Stalag Luft III of *The Great Escape* fame.

The large bathing hall at Grafenwöhr, where fortunate prisoners could have a hot bath.

Russian prisoners at Ohrdruf patiently
awaiting their turn for a bath.

The bathing establishment at Wahn, which was used as a parent camp for the many working parties in its area. Located 20 miles south-east of Cologne, it also contained a punishment barracks for prisoners captured while trying to cross the frontier into Holland.

of being freed from their tormentors, and patiently wait in front of the baths, until their turn comes. Mattresses and clothes are frequently aired and exposed to the rays of the sun in the yards. During the warm season arrangements were made in small rivers and ponds for providing shower and swimming baths for the prisoners. Frequently there are also single baths, particularly in the officer camps.

Mattresses and bedding laid out in the sun to air at Zwickau II, a camp under the jurisdiction of the 19th Army Corps with a capacity of 10,000 prisoners.

Prisoners bathing in the lake at Grafenwöhr in Bavaria.

A shower unit constructed for the prisoners at Grafenwöhr in Bavaria. Such luxuries were the exception rather than the rule.

For the daily wash arrangements are made in all camps. The hair-dressers and barbers amongst the prisoners busily ply their trade. Even the shearing machine has in several instances been employed for removing the savage-like growth of hair and beard. Everywhere provisions are made for the prisoners to wash their linen and underclothing, what they had frequently not been able to do for months before they were taken prisoners.

Wash basins in use at Würzburg, a cathedral town under the jurisdiction of the 2nd Bavarian Army Corps.

Prisoners washing their clothing in the camp at Hahnöfersand near Hamburg.

What German medical science has done in the camps of the prisoners of war will readily bear a comparison with the work of German surgeons and ambulance staffs in the field. According to its size one or several army physicians were appointed, for each prisoners camp. Experienced and renowned medical capacities voluntarily placed their services at the disposal of the Army Board, entirely giving up their private practice. The medical department of the Ministry for War arranged two Sanitary Inspections for the prisoners of war. But also the services of the foreign military surgeons, likewise prisoners, had to be resorted to, as these could better understand their fellow countrymen than the German medical officers. Also the ambulance men were employed everywhere and rendered good services under the supervision of German guards.

Immediately after their arrival all prisoners of war had to submit to being

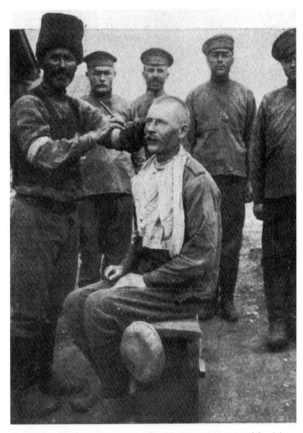

A Russian barber at work at Puchheim camp, near Munich in Bavaria.

Captioned 'washing day at Hammelburg camp' by the German photographer, there appear to be more spectators than workers. The camp was in an ancient town in Bavaria, on the banks of the River Saale.

Russian and French surgeons at the Langensalza camp. With a capacity of 10,000 men, it was the centre for a large number of working parties utilized in the surrounding area.

Hospital and canteen workers at the camp at Grafenwöhr. The hospital was on the outskirts of the town near a new military training ground that would be still in use by NATO troops in 2014.

vaccinated, as well against cholera, as against typhus and against smallpox. This repeated vaccination of hundred thousands of prisoners represented a vastly difficult and expensive task. The ill and seriously wounded are placed in reserve or fortress hospitals, where they are treated and cared for in exactly the same manner as the members of the German army.

When their condition has improved, they are removed to special hospitals for prisoners of war, which are attached to every prisoners' camp. Here also the lighter cases occurring in camp are treated, when it is impossible to treat them in their respective barrack rooms; serious cases, and all those necessitating an extensive operation, are taken to the above mentioned reserve hospitals.

If necessary the prisoners also receive further care beyond the mere nursing, so for example, they are provided with wooden legs, simple, artificial limbs, artificial eyes, false teeth etc. At the present separate camps are being prepared in particularly healthy surrounding for tuberculous prisoners, who are very numerous amongst the sometimes very inferior material, taken as prisoners from the armies of our enemies.

Prisoners at Chemnitz being inoculated against cholera. British prisoners returning from Russian Poland were usually brought back to this camp. Many were employed in neighbouring salt mines.

For officers who are either ill or in need of special care, special sanatoria have been arranged, such as Clausthal and Wildemann in the Hartz, Colberg (Saxe-Meiningen), Augustbad in New Brandenburg, Wahmbeck, Bad Stuer. The two photos from hospital huts show that healthy localities and comfortable beds have been liberally provided, and the view of the bandaging room in the reserve hospital Ingolstadt, shows us that the wounded or sick enemy is treated by physicians and nurses with the same care as their own fellow countrymen. The hospitals are equipped with their own laboratories and dispensaries. And special attention is devoted to the possibility of the convalescents being able to exercise and rest in the large courtyards of the hospital barracks.

Corporal Patrick Durham of the AIF arrived at Grafenwöhr camp in Eastern Bavaria late in the afternoon of 12 September. The camp was built as the training area for the Bavarian army and covered 37 square miles. Durham was taken to a barracks that was being made into a hospital and found that they were the first British troops to arrive there. After three weeks he was inoculated five times for typhus and cholera and was allowed to write letters and postcards home. His parents were overjoyed to hear from him; they had been told that he was missing believed killed.

The French prisoners were very good to the newly-arrived British and shared some of their food parcels with them. Some weeks would pass before Durham would receive his first food parcels from home. In the meantime he tried to stay fit and exercise his injured leg, but his wounds were taking a long time to heal and were continually discharging. His foot was still useless and his name was put forward for eventual repatriation on medical grounds.

The prisoners' infirmary at Ludwigsburg camp.

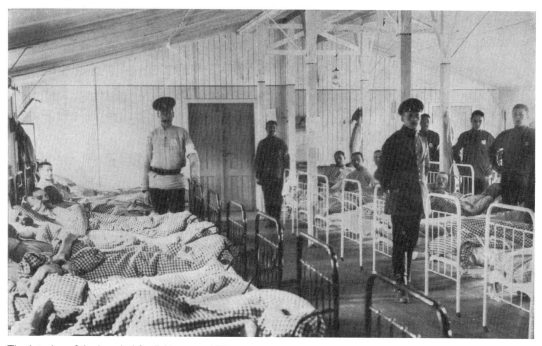

The interior of the hospital for light cases at Bütow camp.

As winter approached the number of wounded British rose to fifty as men were processed for repatriation. The Swiss Commission arrived on 30 October to discuss the exchange of disabled prisoners, but there were others ahead of Durham in the queue. On the positive side of things, food parcels were now arriving including a weekly package from Switzerland of two small loaves of bread and half a pound of cheese. His first parcel from Australia contained

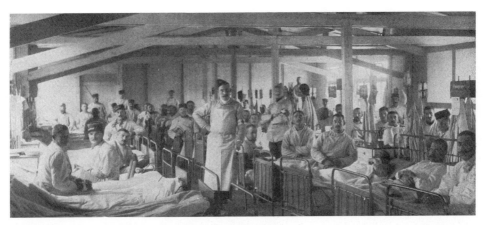

The interior of a large hospital barrack at Friedrichsfeld camp.

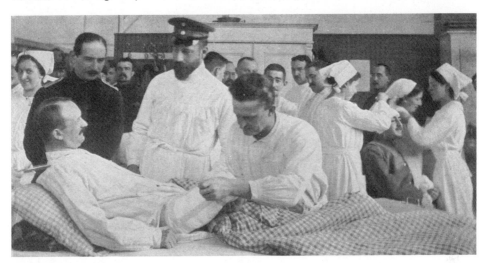

The bandage dressing room at Ingolstadt camp.

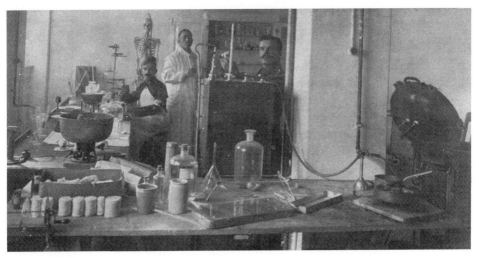

The hospital laboratory in the prisoner-of-war camp at Gütersloh.

The dispensary in the camp at Zossen.

Residents of Reserve Hospital III at Lübeck.

underclothing, socks, scarf, pipe, tobacco and a large bottle of Bovril. The next contained cake, biscuits, tea, cocoa, milk, sugar, jam and fish paste. He shared his good fortune with the other English, Australians, Russians, French and more recently-arrived Moroccan prisoners.

At the end of December Durham slipped and opened up his wound again. It was rather bad luck as it was getting on so well, but his foot was still as dead as a door nail. The doctor spoke to him about having an operation to join the broken nerves, but withdrew the offer a couple of days later. Christmas Day in the hospital was just the same as any other day, although they went to Mass, read by a French soldier priest, in the little church in the hospital. They had

Patients in the hospital grounds at Münster camp.

View of the hospital buildings at Münster camp.

been saving up some of the contents of their food parcels, so had a good feed in their rooms. At night they sang French and English songs for a couple of hours.

At the start of 1915 they began to experience problems with the food parcels. New regulations came in preventing the arrival of civil parcels; they had to come via the Red Cross. In addition, if prisoners wanted tinned goods from their parcels, they had to take a basin to the parcel store where the tin would be opened and the contents deposited into the basin. By now the British and French governments were sending escape aids hidden in items in the parcels, so the Germans were taking more interest in what was being sent to the prisoners.

In March the German doctor once again asked Durham if he would like an operation to try to rejoin the nerves to his foot. He asked the doctor if he could guarantee success and when he said no, Durham refused to let him try. The next month the doctor sent him away to a normal prisoner-of-war camp at Nuremberg. So much for his chances of being repatriated.

One guard was sent with Durham and three other prisoners. He was quite a good fellow who spoke very good English and much of the train ride was spent discussing the war. The Germans were growing anxious for peace and were not as confident of victory as they had been at the start of the war.

The camp was 3 miles from the town and situated on the training grounds of the Nuremberg garrison. The walk to the camp from the station was very hard work and Durham was exhausted when he arrived. Of the 150 English in the camp, only 40 were in residence. The others had been sent out on working parties. Corporals and sergeants did not have to work, although the Russian and French NCOs were given no choice in the matter.

In June 1915 the English sergeants and corporals and the French sergeants were sent to Lechfeld, about 90 miles from Nuremberg. Durham was included in the party and as he could not walk he was pulled in a cart by the prisoners from the station to the camp. He later wrote in his diary:

> The surroundings of the camp is far more pleasant than Nuremberg; we are not boxed up. There are two rows of barbed wire around the camp and on a clear day one can see the mountains of Tyrol which are not far from Switzerland. This place will be alright in summer, but I'm afraid it will be dreadfully cold in winter. We sleep on a straw palaise [sic] which is placed on the floor of course.
>
> There are about 870 French Sergeants here and they say it is a kind of reprisal camp. We don't know how it will effect [sic] the English, as there are only 22 of us. The commandant in charge of the camp is an old man who has been a civil prisoner in England. He was sent back to Germany last year because he was over the age limit. He was 18 years in England and has a son who is a prisoner there. He treats us pretty fair and often comes and has a yarn. He seems to think it is a mistake that we have been sent here, but while we are here we must come under the same rule as the French.

Durham's diary ends here, but he was eventually chosen by the Swiss Medical Commission and was across the border at Constance by October 1917. He was repatriated from Switzerland to England in March 1918. In September he finally boarded a ship bound for Australia.

Private Arthur Gibbons, Canadian Expeditionary Force

The day of 22 April 1915 was one that Private Arthur Gibbons of the Toronto Regiment would remember for the rest of his life. It was the start of the Second Battle of Ypres, the day that the Germans first used poison gas and the day that the 1st Canadian Division suffered terrible casualties. It was also the day that he was hit in the head by a bullet as he was trying to deepen his trench. It was night-time and the Germans were sending up star-shells to illuminate the battlefield. Usually all movement would cease when these flares lit the sky because the enemy snipers were always watching. This time Gibbons was careless, the bullet knocked him to the ground and he was unconscious for two hours.

The Second Battle of Ypres was the only major attack carried out by the Germans on the Western Front in 1915. They were concentrating their forces and their efforts mainly on the Russians on the Eastern Front.

The battle was fought in the infamous Ypres Salient, where the trenches ran in the shape of a giant horseshoe, 5.5 miles long, directly around the city of Ypres. North of the salient, the Belgian army held the line of the Yser, and the northern end of the salient was held by two French divisions. The eastern part of the salient was held by the 1st Canadian Division and two

British divisions. The Germans held the outside flanks of the salient, so the enemy was able to pour fire on the defenders from three sides. For two days prior to the gas attack, the Germans bombarded the city of Ypres and the surrounding villages, killing hundreds of civilians. On the left flank of the salient were the French native troops: Turcos and Algerians from North Africa who were serving in the French army. On the right flank was the Canadian Highland Brigade. In the hamlet of Gravenstafel the Germans released 5,700 canisters containing 168 tons of chlorine gas in front of the French 45th and 87th divisions; Colonial Moroccan and Algerian troops. Clouds 10 to 20ft high and of a greenish-yellow colour enveloped the French trenches. The gas choked and blinded the troops and they began to run away in panic. The gas covered 4 miles of trenches and affected some 10,000 men, half of whom died from asphyxiation or were blinded. Some 2,000 were taken prisoner and the rest fled in terror.

The gas also reached the Highland Brigade, but they did not retire. They were told to urinate on cloth and hold it over their faces to counter the effects of the gas. They extended their lines to the left to try to plug the breach left by the native troops and took heavy casualties with the enemy on three sides. Two Canadian battalions counter-attacked into the gap in the lines but suffered 75 per cent casualties.

Gibbons was lucky that the bullet only creased his head; another half-inch to the left and he would have been killed. However, on the morning of 24 April his luck ran out. The Germans released chlorine gas again, this time directed against the Canadian division situated north-east of Ypres. The Canadians held their ground though, and the fighting was fierce. Gibbons and his comrades were in an isolated position right at the point of the salient and the enemy had surrounded them. There were less than 100 of them left by then and for three hours they fought off seven enemy attacks until they were finally overrun. Gibbons was shot in the leg with an explosive bullet that completely shattered his limb, leaving him lying helpless on the field. A German appeared and was about to bayonet him, when an officer intervened. He questioned him for a couple of minutes and when he realized he was a Canadian, he called him a swine and kicked him. His captors dragged him about 40 yards behind the German trenches and left him lying there for the next four days.

His captors were the 236th Regiment of Saxon Infantry and during the time that he lay there he was stripped of everything that he possessed, including his boots, buttons and shoulder-straps. He was also kicked and beaten and soundly cursed by every German soldier who passed. Eventually he was picked up by German stretcher-bearers and taken to a dressing station in the village of Langemarck. By now British shells were bursting in and around the village, but the Germans made no effort to protect the wounded who were left out in the open. Eventually he was put in a large motor ambulance with German wounded and driven to a hospital.

Two German Army Corps took part in the battle and they penetrated 3 kilometres into allied lines until a British counter-offensive stopped the advance. They had, however, gained the high ground to the north, which significantly weakened the allied position. The fighting continued for another month and by the end of the battle allied losses stood at almost 70,000 compared to 35,000 Germans. The Canadians suffered almost 6,000 casualties.

While the battle continued, Gibbons was sent to a hospital about 15 miles from Ypres, where he was given a preliminary examination and put in a nearby stable with other wounded French and Belgian soldiers. He was left there for twelve days without any medical attention. A rough field dressing had been tied around his wound, a terrible gash on the front and back of his

Austro-Hungarian troops executing Serbian prisoners of war.

shattered thigh bone. Finally, sixteen days after he was wounded, Gibbons was taken into the hospital and laid on the floor to wait his turn on the operating table. He later wrote:

> I saw some awful operations performed. The doctor seemed to have no human feelings at all and treated the wounded German soldiers just as roughly as the wounded prisoners. I saw that doctor amputate a leg and placed it on the ground, not two feet away from me and in plain view. The sight terrified me and made me realize that I could hope for little mercy or kindly treatment from him.

Gibbons was right in his assessment. He was anaesthetized and woke up a few hours later in a bed in one of the wards of the hospital. It was later found when he was X-rayed back in England that the broken bone of his thigh had been completely overlapped, thus causing the injured leg to be 5.5in shorter than the other. His foot and ankle had been turned completely around and when he looked down he saw the bottom of his foot instead of the top. In addition, several nerves in the upper part of his leg had been severed and he had lost the use of the limb entirely. Doctors later contended that it was a deliberate attempt on the part of the Germans to cripple him.

Wittenberg Typhus Outbreak

Wittenberg camp was a miserable place in the wintertime. Built on a flat, sandy plain devoid of trees or shrubs, the camp occupied just over 10 acres and was surrounded by barbed-wire entanglements. The camp itself was divided into eight compounds with six wooden bungalows in each, built to accommodate 120 men per bungalow. However, the camp was full to bursting with 700 to 800 British and a much larger number of French, Belgian and Russian prisoners of war. Instead of holding roughly 6,000 prisoners, the overcrowded buildings held between 15,000 and 17,000 men.

The winter of 1914–15 was extremely cold and the heating arrangements in the bungalows were totally inadequate. Each bungalow contained two stoves but the Germans did not supply enough coal to feed them; in addition, the men were poorly clothed, having lost their greatcoats to their thieving captors months before.

In ideal circumstances, the British prisoners would opt for ventilation and fresh air in their billets, whereas the Russians would close every door and window. However, due to the lack of heating, all prisoners were in agreement that it was best to keep what little warmth they had inside the rooms and every window was kept shut.

Many of their uniforms were in tatters and some men were without boots or socks. They would wrap their feet in straw and walk about with their blankets around them. As there was no wash-house in the camp, there was no means of washing their dirty clothing and to keep themselves clean there was only one trough or tap to each compound, often frozen in wintertime.

The men were also on starvation rations, with black acorn coffee and a 1 kilogram loaf of bread between ten men for breakfast. The bread contained a high percentage of potato and was most unpalatable. The midday meal consisted of a soup made of potato flour, horse beans (broad or fava beans), soya flour, some form of grease and a minimum of meat. Occasionally the midday soup contained a powerfully-smelling sun-dried fish, or at other times dried plums. In the evening there was more thin soup containing margarine. Things would not improve until the first Red Cross food parcels appeared in May of 1915.

As for sleeping arrangements, there was only one mattress between three men and every British prisoner was compelled to share his with one French and one Russian prisoner. The Russians were well-known carriers of lice and in the prevailing conditions in the bungalows, the creatures began to find homes in the clothing of the other prisoners and some of these lice were infected with typhus.

The typhus epidemic broke out in December 1914 and led to the immediate exodus from the camp of the German medical staff, camp guards and officers. The only hospital in the camp comprised two wooden huts capable of holding about 100 patients and they were soon full. There were no British medical officers in the camp when the outbreak started and it was not until February 1915 that six arrived from Halle. They were from a party of thirteen doctors who had been unlawfully imprisoned at Halle since the previous November and were eventually distributed among other German camps.

Majors Fry and Priestley and Captains Sutcliffe, Field, Vidal and Lauder were not told about the epidemic; they only found out from a guard on the train on their way to the camp. They found the British prisoners gaunt, of a particular grey pallor and verminous. Many were lying on the floor in the darkened rooms and others were aimlessly marching up and down. When the medical officers got out into the open air again, Major Fry broke down at the horror of it all.

That evening Captain Vidal and Major Priestley were sent to two temporary hospitals outside the camp, where conditions were better and no infectious diseases were present. The other four officers found themselves responsible for the camp and its sick inmates and of the four, only Captain Lauder would survive.

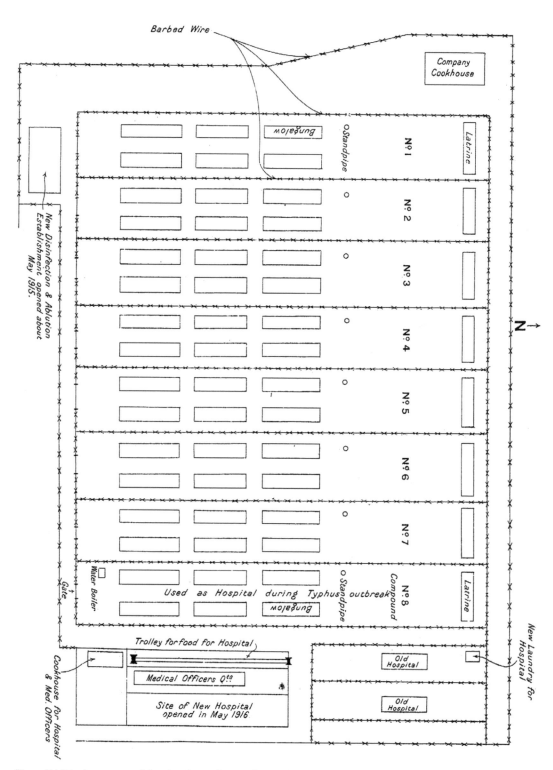

Plan of Wittenberg camp, following the typhus outbreak that claimed the lives of many prisoners.

The symptoms of endemic typhus develop within one or two weeks after initial infection from the bacteria being spread by the lice: high fever, headache, nausea, vomiting, diarrhoea and a rash that covers the whole body. Delays in treatment may allow renal, lung or nervous system problems to develop and between 10 and 60 per cent of those infected may die.

There were no antibiotics available to treat the disease. Good sanitation, boiling of clothing and extermination of the lice were the only options open to the doctors and none of these choices were immediately available.

The camp hospital was overflowing with sick men and dozens of others were scattered among the bungalows, sharing infected mattresses with their companions. There were no stretchers available and the sick men had to be transported to the hospital on the tables on which the men would eat their food. There were no mattresses in the hospital and the diet for the sick was totally inadequate: half a petit pain and half a cup of milk per day, plus soup from the kitchens that came up in a wooden tub without a cover and was full of dirt and dust.

Two Russian medical generals were in command in the hospital at that time. There were about 1,000 cases of typhus in the camp and others were coming down with it at the rate of around 50 per day, with 150 British among the total.

Major Fry and Captain Sutcliffe died of typhus about a month after their arrival and Captain Field succumbed some time later. Captain Lauder was stricken with the disease on 7 March but eventually recovered. On the day that Lauder went down with the disease, Major Priestley and Captain Vidal arrived back at the camp.

When Major Priestley made his rounds of the bungalows, he saw delirious men waving arms brown to the elbow with faecal matter. The patients were alive with vermin and there were no bedpans so the state of the mattresses was indescribable. Bedsores were common and in several cases toes or whole feet became gangrenous and sufficient bandages were not available to dress them. One prisoner, a private in the Royal Scots Fusiliers, had both legs amputated below the knee due to gangrene.

One way to halt the spread of the disease was to disinfect the lice-ridden clothing of the men, but only a small sulphur chamber was available. As there was little spare clothing to go round, if a prisoner gave up his clothing for disinfecting he would have to remain naked until it was returned to him. It was impossible to wash the patients properly as the Germans refused to supply any soap, but Captain Vidal eventually obtained a supply from England.

Major Priestley took over treatment of typhus in the hospital and Captain Vidal was put in charge of the surgical ward. When Captain Lauder had recovered, he was made responsible for the observation ward in Compound Number 8. After much arguing with their captors, Major Priestley arranged for all British typhus cases to be collected in one bungalow of the compound and he badgered the Germans for bedding, clothing, urinals, etc. and improved the food supply for the patients. Things slowly began to improve.

During the whole period of the outbreak, the German medical officer Dr Aschenbach only entered the camp once, about a month after Major Priestley took charge. He arrived wearing a complete suit of protective clothing including a mask and rubber gloves. The inspection was brief and he departed as quickly as he had come. It is reported that he was later awarded the Iron Cross for his work in combating the outbreak.

After the middle of April beds and clothing began to arrive for the hospital and with the warmer weather the number of cases decreased. The last British case occurred in the middle of May and the last Russian case in July. Of the 250 to 300 British cases, 60 of them died. The numbers of French and Russian dead were much greater.

Eventually the Germans built a steam clothing sterilizer outside the camp and several new hospital bungalows were constructed, but it was too little and too late.

In 1916 the Government Committee on the Treatment by the Enemy of British Prisoners of War concluded that the cruel administrators of Wittenberg camp were to blame for the extent of the outbreak and the many deaths due to lack of treatment. Prior to the outbreak the prisoners were badly treated by the guards and floggings and beatings were commonplace. Some men were tied to posts with their arms above their heads for hours.

When representatives from the American Embassy visited the camp in the October they noted that the prisoners were reluctant to speak to them in case of retribution once they had gone. The blame was laid at the door of the camp commandant General Zincke von Dassel.

Limburg was another camp to avoid. Some 2,000 Irish prisoners were sent there, in order to be persuaded to join Roger Casement's Irish Brigade. Very few took up the offer and a starvation regime was instituted to try to persuade others to follow. Private P. Cullen of the 2nd Munster Fusiliers later reported:

> Private Murphy, Irish Guards, attempted to commit suicide by cutting his throat and Private Joyce became insane and was removed to an asylum. Several others also became insane but I cannot remember their names. I was in the camp hospital from 25th September 1915 until 25th May 1916 having contracted consumption, which was caused by ill-treatment, starvation and contact with other men who already had the disease.

Kriegsgefangenenlager Limburg.

Limburg prisoner-of-war camp, used as a concentration point for the Irish soldiers who the Germans hoped to persuade to fight against the British in Ireland.

French cemetery at Wittenberg camp, following the typhus epidemic.

The medical treatment was bad, owing to lack of medical stores. Wounded men suffered especially owing to the insufficiency of bandages. While I was in the hospital 100 prisoners died of consumption. There were German orderlies in attendance on the sick, but they did very little work; all the work was done by the patients. The hospital buildings were huts of the same sort as those in the camp. The food was better than it was in the camp. Bread rations consisted of two small rolls of white bread per day. At mid-day about 4 ounces of meat were served to each man with the soup. We also received boiled rice and fruit and milk (condensed) at 4 pm every day. Sanitary arrangements were satisfactory and all nationalities were treated alike. The chief doctor, Dr Liever, was very good to us, but was unable to give us proper treatment as he was not supplied with the necessary medical stores. Hospital suit, shirt and slippers were supplied to all men in hospital and the sheets were changed every week.

Chapter 7

Arbeits Kommandos and Reprisals

Seaman Byrne (see Chapter 3, 'Sunk at Jutland') eventually found himself on a working party in a forest, felling trees and trimming the branches. He was determined to do as little work as possible for the enemy, but eventually fell foul of the civilian overseer. Sent back to Brandenburg he was given ten days in the 'strafe camp' which meant hard work on bread and water. He was forced to carry heavy sacks of wheat from canal barges to a shed. He only just managed to carry out the work and was on the verge of collapsing when he was transferred to lighter work until his punishment was complete.

Two days later, Byrne and his fellow workers were sent to a coal mine near the Bohemian frontier, miles away from the nearest town. They lived in a small wooden shed, just large enough to hold them all when they were in bed. The beds as usual were just loose straw and one blanket, and with snow now on the ground it was bitterly cold.

Byrne was given a shovel and told to fill fifteen tubs a day with coal, a laborious job that took from 6 am to 10 pm every day. However, as he was the smallest there, they gave him a different job, pushing tubs of coal onto an overhead wire that took them to a factory about 2 miles away. The other fellows suggested that he should cause the wires to break over the field by putting the tubs too close to each other. He thought that an excellent idea, so one night he put three tubs on close to each other and waited. He did not have to wait long, as there was a crash and he realized that he had been successful. The civilian workers were extremely angry though, and gave him a severe beating. However, the mine was out of action for twenty-four hours and his pals all clapped him on the back.

Some 200 yards away there was another mine with prisoners of war working. They heard that one of the prisoners had been shot dead because he hit the civilian who was bullying him. Thereafter they decided to be more careful and not push their luck any further.

Carrying out acts of sabotage was a risky business. If a man was caught red-handed, the chances were that he would be shot. However, it was impressed upon the troops that in the event of their capture, it was their duty to try to escape or to inflict as much damage on the enemy as possible. In order to assist and encourage the prisoners, various devices were created and sent to the camps hidden in food or clothing parcels. The French were particularly creative in this respect.

Instructions were sent to the prisoners working on farms on how to disrupt the German potato crops:

Pick out infected potatoes, those with black spots. Slightly scratch the skin near the shoot of the ones left for sowing and rub together the scratch with the black spots of a bad potato. In this way the 'rotting agent' is transferred from a bad potato to the shoot of a healthy one. Better still, remove the shoot altogether with your finger nails, knife, a piece of wood, or the 'extirpateur' which will be sent to you in cake, chocolate etc.

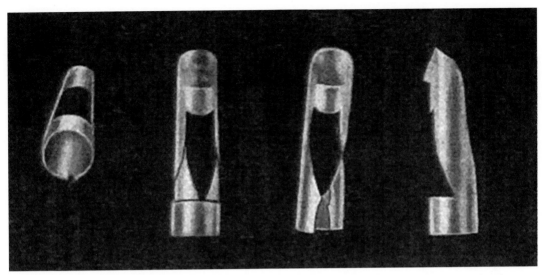

'Extirpateurs' sent to French prisoners of war for use in removing the eyes of potatoes and ruining the next year's crop.

This specially-produced 'extirpateur' was a piece of tin tubing 3 to 4cm long, with one end cut at an angle leaving sharp edges; it was designed to be fastened to a thin piece of wood, cut at the top at an angle. To use the tool: 'Push the extirpateur into a potato near the shoot, twist and pull out the shoot. All this you must do in such a way, that it is not noticed by the Germans. A poor harvest is for them like a lost battle.' It was also suggested that prisoners working on farms try to mix infected potatoes with the healthy ones and that scratching the skin of a healthy potato would help it to rot more easily.

All sorts of devices were designed to be smuggled into the prison camps inside the covers of books, or in tins or packets of food. As previously mentioned, the Germans would eventually counter this by ordering prisoners to open the food containers in front of them and even decant the contents into a tin or bowl so the food had to be eaten right away.

Special types of shoe polish were sent out, with instructions on using the 'polish' to grease the bearings of machinery to induce wear and eventual failure. It was recommended that sand could be mixed with grease to achieve the same thing. There were small glass capsules, the contents of which could be used for arson. There were powders and pastilles that could be used for poisoning cattle. Special powders were sent to the prisoners, which could be dissolved in water and used to write 'invisible' letters.

This innocent-looking tin of boot polish contains a substance used to grease bearings to accelerate their failure.

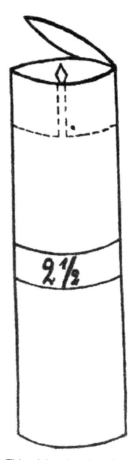

This delayed-action fuse with 2½ minutes marked on it could be used to set fire to barns, etc.

If a member of a working party tried to set fire to a barn, for instance, the chances are that he would be found out. Therefore delayed-action special fuses, burning glasses, methylated spirits in solid form and firelighters that could be used as fuses were sent out hidden in food parcels. One such item was a capsule of black cardboard, with a narrow band around the middle with 2½ or 3½ written on it. Under the lid was a piece of glass with a pointed top, protruding through a piece of cardboard seal on the inside of the capsule. Below that was a glass container with some liquid inside. The instructions read: 'After opening the upper lid, break the top of the glass, place the capsule upright among some easily inflammable material. After the number of hours shown on the outside of the capsule have elapsed, the liquid in the container, now exposed to air, bursts into flames lasting about five minutes.'

Prisoners were also encouraged to try to undermine German morality by engaging in sexual activity with German women and girls. Most prisoners did not have the opportunity and their priorities were usually somewhat different from those of normal civilian life; food, rest, warmth and security generally came first. No doubt prisoners working in close contact with females on farms, in factories, etc. may have had the opportunity but there is no way of knowing how successful this directive was.

Not all prisoners were lucky enough to be shipped off to a prisoner-of-war camp in Germany. Some were used as slave labour in the rear areas, where they faced the same risks as the German soldiers. Second Lieutenant H.S. Ward of the Royal Flying Corps (RFC) was shot down near Lille and received a bullet in his left leg. On 23 December 1915 he was taken by train to Valenciennes Lazarette, which had previously been a hospital or a school. He recalled that the surgical treatment was not good, but it was at least humane. He was put in a room with about thirty others, including twenty Russians who had supposedly suffered accidents in the factories but were more probably wounded while digging second-line trenches for the Germans. Thousands of British prisoners are believed to have perished while working close to the front lines.

In the early summer of 1915, thirty-five British officers were sent to Cologne to be imprisoned in cells as a reprisal against the alleged maltreatment of German submarine crews. The majority of the officers went from Crefeld and when the reprisal ended two months later they returned looking very white and ill.

On 8 May 1916 1,000 NCOs and men left Döberitz prisoner-of-war camp for Russia. Another 1,000 men were gathered at Frankfurt am Oder and they followed three days later. The men were divided into 500-strong working parties, one of which was Number 4 Company, employed in the docks at Libau from 14 May 1916 to February 1917. On 23 February the company left Libau for Mitau and two days later things changed for the worse. Their destination that day was the village of Latchen, near Kelzien, a march of 25 kilometres (15 miles) away and a hard slog for a fit infantryman, let alone 500 half-starved prisoners of war. The party was escorted by a squadron of Uhlans, mounted lancers who drove the party along in the most brutal manner, and many fell out or staggered along, being driven by the lances and whips of their captors. Only eighty of the men reached the village in any sort of formation.

The accommodation at their new camp was one huge tent about 70 metres long by 7 metres wide and all 500 men were expected to live in it. Pitched on a frozen swamp, there was no fuel for heating the tent and no proper means of obtaining water for cooking or washing. The rations were barely enough to keep the men alive; there were no food parcels and smoking was not allowed. They were not far from the front lines and occasional Russian shells exploded nearby.

Company Sergeant Major A. Gibb of the 2nd Argyll and Sutherland Highlanders was the senior NCO in charge of two of the companies. He later reported:

The Germans read out an Order, stating that the British had been brought to this place as a reprisal for the employment of German prisoners in France, where they were being ill-treated, starved and made to work under fire. The orders of the guard stated that no mercy was to be shown to the prisoners, every one of whom had assisted in halting the Kaiser's Army from reaching Paris.

The working parties were constantly under Russian shell fire, but there was little rifle or machine gun fire. The treatment was so brutal that the men soon became mere living skeletons, too weak to move about. Nevertheless, they were kicked and beaten out to work morning after morning by the medical Feldwebel; their comrades had to help them to walk out, lead them about all day and very often carry them home at night. Hospital accommodation was quite inadequate in the camp and medical comforts or attention was

The burial in May 1917 of Private John Grant of the Hampshire Regiment at Libau in Russia. This was one of the punishment working parties employed just behind the German lines in Russia; many of the men died and were buried there.

British prisoners used to build airplane hangars at Altburg in Russia.

almost non-existent. The result, in figures, was that 14 men died at the camp and eight more in the hospital at Mitau, all from exhaustion and starvation except one who was murdered. The medical facilities at the hospital were non-existent and the personnel consisted mainly of Russian deserters and prisoners. The weather started to improve in April and the first consignment of food parcels were issued. Around 20,000 food parcels had accumulated at Mitau, many looted by the Germans or containing food that had perished. If the Germans had issued them to the prisoners, it would have probably saved the 23 lives.

The camp was broken up on 10th June 1917 and after a month's rest at Libau, the party was employed in light work and occupied good quarters until November 1917, when it was sent back to Germany. 276 NCOs and men returned from the front lines out of the original 500. Of the remainder most had already been sent back to Germany incapacitated for any other work, some of these for the remainder of their lives.

On 21 December 1916, the German army demanded that the French withdraw the German prisoners in their hands to a distance of 30 kilometres from the front line near Verdun. If the French did not comply by 15 January 1917, the Germans threatened to build their own camps within reach of French artillery fire.

When no reply was received, the Germans built a small prison camp at Flabas. It was only 50 metres long and 30 metres wide and fenced with barbed wire. The only barrack hut in the camp could only accommodate 200 of the 500 men imprisoned there; 300 had to remain out in the open air, even in wintertime.

The guard force comprised one German officer, a *Feldwebel*, two *Unteroffiziere* and forty stormtroopers and they instigated a brutal regime against the luckless prisoners. The guards used their clubs on the prisoners for the smallest excuse and they were put on starvation rations. On four days of the week they only received one small piece of bread, yet they were used for forced labour from dawn till dusk. They had to build roads in the line of fire in the Bois des Caures and in the direction of the lines of Samogneux and at the end of the day parties of ten prisoners were forced to carry water 600 metres in the line of fire of the French guns.

Finally, after several months the French authorities met the demands of the German government. The camp at Flabas was abandoned and the prisoners withdrawn to camps near Montmédy and Longuyon. Only 300 of the 500 French prisoners survived the treatment at this camp.

This photo appears to show a British working party band near Windau (Ventspils) in Latvia, Russia. They seem to have an armband marked EKI or EKI on their right sleeve.

A prisoner-of-war working party and their guards at Mannheim on the right bank of the River Rhine in 1915. In 1917 it was used as a clearing camp for prisoners due for exchange or repatriation.

Chapter 8

Keeping Idle Hands Busy

Occupation

From the book *1915*:

In the prisoners camps it has been observed, more than anywhere else, that work is the blessing of mankind and that idleness leads to vice. After the terrors of the war the rest in the prisoners' camp, at first, had a calming, quieting effect. But the idle life, the comparatively close confinement and at the same time, the longing after their homes, must necessarily soon have a depressing effect on such strong young men. The better elements amongst the prisoners therefore, very soon, applied voluntarily for some kind of occupation or work, which was willingly offered to them, to their own benefit besides, as they could thereby earn a trifle and improve their own conditions. When starting out to work, therefore, we observe them mostly showing a happy, cheerful mien.

First of all work was provided for prisoners in agriculture, in order to find substitutes for the many millions of men who have answered the call of their country and are fighting

A Russian working party from Langensalza camp.

A French working party prepares to march out from the Dülmen camp. The camp was 5 miles from the town and was the centre for a large number of working parties.

A working party of mixed nationalities in a village near Landshut.

under the colours. Prisoners of war are sent in troops from ten men upwards with Landsturm men as guards, to work in estates and communities, and these troops may, within each community, be further subdivided. When prisoners of war are employed for agricultural work, the employer provides housing and food and a daily pay of 30 Pfennigs. With many more employers however, prisoners may earn, by diligence and skill, far more, either by receiving additional allowances or by doing piece work. Prisoners were also employed in large numbers for amelioration work, chiefly in cultivating moors. Woods are cleared, trees are cut down and the land prepared for further cultivation. Laden with wood for kitchens and stoves we frequently see the workers returning home from work. Also in road and railway construction the prisoners of war have been employed on an extensive scale. Many thousands of them have found work in mining and industrial plants, earning their high wages, which they either spend for their own comfort, or save up for the time when they shall be returning home again.

The work performed by prisoners of war may be divided into two general classes, viz such for private persons in industry and agriculture, and in work for the common benefit. It may be admitted that the prisoners of war have filled many a gap torn by the conscription of all men eligible for the army. Thousands of acres of moor and virgin soil have been cultivated by prisoners, many miles of high roads and railways have been constructed by them, canals have been dug and other public buildings and work have been completed.

The camp routine calls for a large number of prisoners, for peeling potatoes, for piling them in stores, for growing vegetables or caring for ornamental gardens, above all, however, in the camp cobblers shop or in the tailors' or carpenters' department. The Russian prisoners of war are very skilled in wicker work and carving; also straw plaiting

Prisoners spreading manure on the fields near Friedrichsfeld.

Russian prisoners from Löcknitz cultivating the moors close to the German-Polish border.

Russian prisoners digging trenches near Wasbek in the extreme north of Germany.

Prisoners from the camp at Münster chopping firewood.

Russian prisoners clearing brushwood and trees near Wasbek.

Weary Russian prisoners returning to the camp at Grafenwöhr.

work is performed. Cement workers devoted their skills towards decorating the camp and making articles for sale. Amongst the Russians, mosaic workers decorated their camp with various specimens of their handsome work. Also sculptors and painters, and above all amateurs amongst the officer prisoners, endeavoured to make use of their art, and in many a camp an exhibition of artistic work could be held, and quite respectable articles were made for sale in the various studios, which brought the maker a very welcome income. Many prisoners of war may also be employed for various kinds of profitable work outside their internment camps.

Prisoners of war using
their mechanical skills.

Prisoners of war preparing potatoes for storage at Bütow camp in Mecklenburg in the north-east of Germany.

Prisoners tending a rather small garden at Grafenwöhr in Bavaria.

A boot repair shop in Eichstatt camp in Bavaria.

Prisoners working in a tailor's shop in Güstrow camp.

Prisoners working in a carpenter's shop in Cassel.

Wicker-workers and carvers working at Aschaffenburg.

Russian Mohammedans producing street signs in the carpenter's shop at Zossen.

Prisoners working at the labour-intensive straw-plaiting shop in Gross Portisch camp.

Captioned by the Germans as 'two artists in cement work' in Heuberg camp in 1915. They appear to be taking care of the pigs at the same time. This place in Baden-Württemberg would become one of the Nazis' first concentration camps in 1933.

An artistic garden created in Neuhammer camp in Upper Silesia. Some 100,000 men were registered to the camp, but most were away on working parties.

French prisoners in a sculptor's shop in Zossen camp.

Prisoners trying their hand at painting in the camp at Celle.

Russian prisoners in the painters' shop at Stargard. The camp also had basket-weaving workshops and was administered by the 2nd Army Corps.

A prisoners' arts and crafts exhibition at Friedrichsfeld camp.

Entertainments

For whiling away the leisure hours after work and for breaking the monotony of camp life, besides for occupying those unable to work, in some other manner, all kinds of entertainments had to be devised. In the officers camps, and also in many soldiers' camps, the suggestions came from the prisoners of war themselves. But in many instances the commandants and the German staff of guards had to approach the prisoners with suggestions and assistance. Music and singing afforded the best pastime, both whiling away the time to the performers and delighting their comrades, as listeners. Musical bands were formed everywhere, instruments were supplied to them; in some officers' camps there is even a piano. In other camps orchestras have been formed, playing self-made instruments or under a German bandmaster. The Sunday Concert in the Chemnitz camp shows that not only the prisoners, but also the German officers and subalterns form a grateful audience. In the hospitals the performances of the camp band are welcomed for the entertainment and the cheering of the wounded and sick.

Prisoners, who are not commissioned off to work, must keep themselves healthy and fresh by drill and exercise under their own subalterns. Gymnastics are busily practiced. Also jumping and tennis. Regular competitions, races etc are arranged, and the group of competitors, ready for the start in the officers' camp Werl, promises a good sport. Football is, of course, popular with all nations, and in particular with the British prisoners, but also ball games and skittles are eagerly played. The Russians delight in showing themselves off at their national dances, and the British prisoners at Ruhleben could not live without regular boxing matches. Croquette, Lotto and Chess are also very popular. Games at cards may only be played under supervision, in order that there should be no gambling.

The orchestra in the officers' camp at Halle.

An orchestra with self-made instruments in the camp at Stuttgart, the capital of Württemberg.

A prisoners' orchestra at Danzig-Troyl camp.

A Sunday concert by a prisoners' orchestra at Chemnitz.

A concert by a French orchestra at Göttingen camp.

The Bing Boys at Güstrow officers' camp. (*Australian War Memorial*)

Russian prisoners undergoing physical exercise at Zittau (Gross Poritsch) camp.

Russian prisoners undergoing physical exercise at Gross Poritsch camp.

The French gymnastic club at Erfurt camp.

A gymnastic performance at the prisoner-of-war camp in Stuttgart II. There were two camps in the city: one in an abandoned factory building and one 3 miles away in a disused factory on a slope overlooking the town.

Jumping exercise in the French civilian internees' camp at Rastatt.

Prisoners playing football on the exercise ground in Celle. The camp would be broken up in the autumn of 1916.

French civilian prisoners on the start line for a running race in the internees' camp at Rastatt.

The running race course in the internees' camp at Rastatt.

Athletic sports: Winners and Sports Committee in Werl, a camp in a Franciscan monastery.

British prisoners half-heartedly appearing to be playing football in Schneidemühl camp.

French prisoners playing boules in their camp at Eichstatt.

Prisoners playing a game with skittles in Landshut.

British civilian internees in the camp at Ruhleben square off in the boxing ring.

Russian dancers show their skills in the prisoner-of-war camp at Czersk in West Prussia.

Above: Recreation time for prisoners in Königsbrück camp.

Left: Prisoners playing lotto in the camp at Ohrdruf.

Russian prisoners playing cards in Heuberg camp.

Pictorial arts at the prisoners' camps have produced many noteworthy specimens, as may be seen from our illustrations. The views from the officer prisoners' camp at Marienberg and the soldiers' camp Grafenwöhr show that the prisoners suffer no lack of opportunity for walks. The group of British prisoners of war at Schneidemühl, certainly, does not make a disconsolate impression. The photograph from the Heuberg camp shows that the prisoners occupy much of their leisure hours with reading and handwork. In civil internment camps there are of course children's playgrounds, so that the little mites should miss nothing. The German subaltern officers are, besides, their special friends and protectors, and bring them many a cake of chocolate.

Religious Service

In the German prisoner of war camps we find representatives of almost all religions and creeds in the world, and all have been afforded the opportunity of enjoying the blessings of their respective religions. Existing churches were, as for example in the civilian camp at Traunstein, placed at their disposal, or special churches were arranged, as in the Senne camp. Available huts in camp have, in other cases, been equipped by the prisoners in a worthy manner to serve as church or chapel, according to the wishes of the respective ministers. The interior view of the Russian or of the French church in the prisoners camp at Königstein, certainly, is a very impressive one. A synagogue is also provided for Jewish prisoners.

The large number of prisoners often renders it necessary to hold field services, which do not lack the necessary solemnity. The divine service in the civilian camp at Rastatt has gained a special interest by the presence of the children and nurses. And that, as shown in

The prisoners' theatre in Celle.

The prisoners' theatre at Amberg camp on the outskirts of the town near the Bavarian army barracks.

A prisoners' play being rehearsed at Münster I camp. There were four camps near Münster, numbered one to four. This camp was some distance from the city in open country.

Clowns performing for the prisoners in Stuttgart II, situated in a disused factory overlooking the town.

the photograph from Heuburg, a German Prince, H.R.H. Prince Max of Saxony, addresses the Russian prisoners of war in their own language, is, undoubtedly, without its equivalent in enemy countries.

Four photographs from various camps show how military honours and a solemn funeral are accorded to prisoners of war, who have died in captivity. The deceased are interred either at the neighbouring cemeteries, or, in larger camps, at special graveyards arranged for the purpose, and the prisoners do not fail, and are even assisted by the camp commandants, in erecting permanent memorials to their late comrades.

The programme for entertainments to be staged by French actors at Stuttgart II.

Open-air theatre at the hospital on the outskirts of Grafenwöhr.

French prisoners taking exercise at the camp at Grafenwöhr.

British prisoners outside one of their huts at Schneidemühl.

Above: The children's playground in the French civilian internees' camp at Rastatt.

Left: Prisoners returning from church at Traunstein. The camp was located in south-east Bavaria in a former salt-producing facility.

Prisoners on their way to church in the camp at Sennelager II.

The interior of the prisoners' chapel at Zwickau II camp.

The interior of the Russian church at Königstein, a fortress high above the River Elbe near the Saxo-Bohemia frontier.

The interior of the French church at Königstein.

The synagogue in Zwickau II.

Captioned by the Germans as a 'Greek Ritual Service' at Sprottau. Close by was a lazarette of forty barracks for tubercular prisoners.

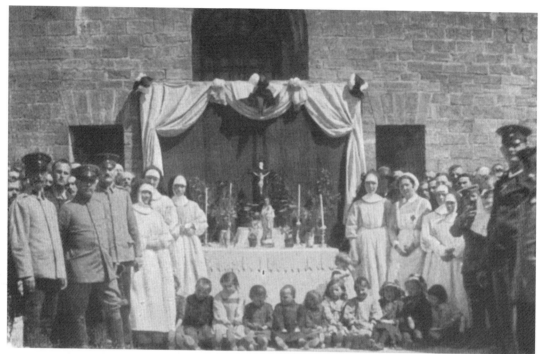

A Catholic divine service for French civilian internees at Rastatt.

The prisoner-of-war church in Minden camp.

A Russian divine service at Görlitz.

A Jewish divine service at Hammerstein.

An orthodox service at the side of the river at Danzig-Troyl.

A Mahometan service at Zossen.

His Royal Highness Prince Max of Saxony preaches to Russian prisoners in their own language at Heuburg.

The funeral of a Russian prisoner at Königsbrück.

French prisoners lay one of their comrades to rest at Ohrdruf.

German guards fire a salute at the funeral of a prisoner of war at Rastatt.

The funeral procession for a deceased prisoner of war at Rastatt.

Instruction

The care for the prisoners of war also extends to their spiritual needs, and very generously, they are allowed as free a scope as possible.

As they are entirely cut off from the outer world, it was necessary to enable them to follow the progress of the historic happenings in which they had participated, and to occupy their mind in other ways.

The German Army Board supplies them with newspapers in their own language and also allows them to read the German dailies. Contrary to other enemy countries, Germany laid stress upon the fact the prisoners of war should find in all these papers, also those in foreign languages, the unabbreviated official reports of all belligerent countries. This impartiality at first, indeed, after certain reports of victories gained by the French and Russians, caused some excitement amongst the prisoners, but gradually, with the assistance of maps from the theatre of war, the conviction gained that the German reports were the most reliable of all. The disappointment which followed was a lesson, which though hard, was still necessary and beneficial. Just those misleading reports of our adversaries are our greatest enemy. And has Germany not all cause to defend herself against them?

Taken from the turmoil of the battle and transferred into the quiet calm of camp life, removed from the nerve-exciting, poisoning atmosphere of enmity, quiet consideration would spread amongst them. Slowly and steadily it gained on the minds of the prisoners of war that the land of the Huns, Germany, about which they had been told the most fearful and terrible tales only, was actually a land of order, reliability, high culture and beauty, a land, which as they say themselves, is full of features well worth copying. 'No-one ever told us that', they exclaimed, when it was mentioned to them.

And so the desire grew in them to get to know the country of their captivity still better. The number of applications, asking for book on Germany grew to such an extent that the wish was gladly granted, and libraries were established in all prisoners' camps; but this was not all. Schools were opened at which, besides writing, reading and arithmetics in their own language, also the German language is taught and instructive papers are read. Also the cinematograph is made to serve the purpose. The stirring, active cultural life in Germany, into which the prisoners of war were inevitably drawn, awakened in them the desire for an increased activity of the mind. Newspapers in all languages were created amongst themselves, self-written plays were studied and performed on the various stages in the camps. Singers, choirs, orchestras bring life into the wooden towns and beside the beautiful, fiery songs of the Latin nations, the deeply felt, Slavic tunes very frequently the German national songs are heard, sung by the 'enemy'.

We must here also with sincere gratitude mention beside other benevolent institutions, the very active share the Young Men's Christian Association has taken in the care of the prisoners of war. With its ample means it has constructed special assembly huts with reading and writing rooms – Prisoners' Homes, which enabled the revival of spiritual life amongst the prisoners. All this is willingly conceded and promoted by the German authorities; in the hope that reciprocity will thereby be secured in the enemy countries, and the same facilities and leniencies will be afforded in the wellbeing of German prisoners of war abroad.

The reading room in the camp at Göttingen, an old university town. Classes and lectures were held in the camp under Professor Stange of the university.

The reading room at Cassel, where some 20,000 prisoners were held in wooden barracks.

The apparently well-stocked library at Ohrdruf.

In the dining room of the officers' camp at Halle.

Left: Prisoners inspecting the photographer's camera at Grafenwöhr.

Below: The library at Heuberg camp.

Friedrichsfeld

Prisoners here had a good football ground which they could use every afternoon and they were allowed to play any indoor games, although gambling was forbidden. A library was started when they began to receive books from England, although only books published prior to the war could be sent. Their own NCOs held a parade for physical drill every morning. There was also a school for men who could not work. They were taught tin-smithing, wood-carving, printing, teaching of French and Russians, also the means for learning music, book-binding and carpentry. A corporal took religious service every Wednesday and Sunday and a Padre Williams held a service on several occasions. A German padre also took an extra service on two occasions, but confined his remarks to religious questions.

A comfortable life was offered to many of the 10,000 Irish men serving in the British army who were taken prisoner. These were men of the Royal Dublin Fusiliers who were surrounded and captured at the battle of Le Cateau on 26 August 1914; Connaught Rangers of whom 280 were taken at Le Grand Fayt the same day; Royal Munster Fusiliers, of whom 300 were captured the next day at Étreux when the 2nd Battalion was almost wiped out; and men from the Leinster and Royal Irish Regiments forced to surrender in October 1914.

In Ireland an insurgency was gathering pace, with the intention of freeing that country from British rule. One of the leaders, Roger Casement, approached the German government about raising an Irish Brigade from the prisoners of war to fight against the British in Ireland. To that end Irish prisoners were sent to Limburg camp, with around 2,200 there by the start of 1915. The Germans hoped that improved conditions would persuade the men to change sides, but the majority of them were having none of it. The Germans had killed many of their comrades and Casement received a rough reception.

Private William Dooley, 2nd Royal Irish, records that Casement made a recruiting speech and all the Irish were gathered together around a provision box. Casement got up on this and made a long speech: 'The men were very restless during the speech, but they restrained themselves to the end. Then, as Casement passed away, they let themselves go, hushing, hissings, and calling him all sorts of names.'

The punishment for these loyal Irishmen was severe. It is believed that the deliberately harsh regime and starvation rations were aimed at persuading the prisoners to join Casement. Private William O'Connell later commented: 'No tents were erected, and we had only the blue sky above us. In hail, rain, frost and snow we were condemned to this terrible ordeal. During all

Friedrichsfeld camp with gardens planted between the barracks.

the time the condition of the men was something awful and we encountered savagery and brutality of the worst kind.' Many men died from starvation and a cross was later erected at the camp, listing the names of forty-five Irish prisoners of war who died at the camp. Two of them – Patrick Moran of the Connaught Rangers and William Devlin of the Royal Munster Fusiliers – had been shot by the guards. The causes of death among PoWs vary from camp to camp and vary throughout the war. Tuberculosis became a problem at Limburg. A small number died through accidents and some were shot by guards. Many died as a result of lack of care and medical attention. The figures for British prisoners of war who died in PoW camps were 172 officers and 6,249 other ranks. A figure of 3 per cent has been quoted for British prisoners of war who died in German hands.

In the end only fifty-five men joined Casement's cause and they were moved to Zossen in July. One more volunteer would join them in the winter of 1915. They were supposed to be billeted with the German 203rd Infantry Regiment with whom they were to train as machine-gunners, but first of all went to Halbmondlager, a show camp 3 miles away for coloured prisoners of war. Casement was eventually landed back in Ireland by submarine, but was soon discovered and arrested.

With the failure of the Easter Rising and the capture of Casement, the Germans gave up on the idea of an Irish Brigade. The Irishmen lost their machine guns, and their instructors from the Prussian Grenadier Guards were sent back to their unit. In July 1916 the men were sent to a camp at Danzig-Troyl, still dressed in their green Irish Brigade uniforms and the NCOs still wearing their sidearms. Soon most of them were sent out to work on farms or factories in the surrounding area and eventually the sidearms and uniforms would go too. As for Casement, he would later be hanged following the failed Easter Rising in 1916.

A photo of some of the small number of rebel Irish soldiers to join Casement's Irish Brigade at Limburg camp.

Giessen camp Catholic prisoner-of-war choir.

Conditions in Giessen camp appear to have been a little better. There was a Catholic choir and drama club within the camp and the men appear to have had plenty of leisure time.

'As prison camps go, Giessen is a good one,' wrote Private Simmons, a Canadian PoW in Giessen. 'The place is well drained; the water is excellent; the sanitary conditions are good, too; the sleeping accommodations are ample, there being no upper berths such as exist in all the other camps I have seen. It is the "show-camp", to which visitors are brought, who then, not having had to eat the food, write newspaper articles telling how well Germany treats her prisoners. If these people could see some of the other camps that I have seen, the articles would have to be modified.'

Chapter 9

Escape

Escape organizations existed in most prisoner-of-war camps. They were there to assist anyone wishing to try to regain his freedom and could provide a number of aids to help them. Essential items such as compasses or maps could be sent hidden in food parcels but clothing, food, false passes, etc. had to be procured or manufactured within the camp. There were many types of uniforms being worn in the camps and often they could be modified to resemble German uniforms or civilian clothes.

Two French officers escaped by dressing as German soldiers. Russian caps were made to look like German caps by sewing on red stripes and forged cockades. Belts, bayonets and tassels were also created and a French field grey coat was fitted with German epaulettes. An English captain converted his sleeveless 'Havelock' coat into an army coat, complete with buttons made from tin. He found a black leather belt and made a bayonet holder to fit on it. The bayonet itself was skilfully carved from a piece of wood. Eventually, disguised as a *Landsturm* (militia) home guard, with two other officers disguised as German orderlies pushing the camp post cart, they walked past the guards and out of the camp.

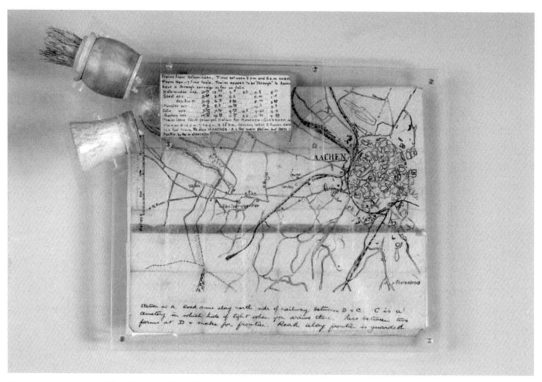

The escape map used by Major J. Shaw hidden in his shaving soap brush.

Once out of the camp, there were many other obstacles to face. Clothing had to fit in with what the locals were wearing; passes were necessary, especially for train travel or for identification; German money and a supply of food was always handy; and a good map, updated with known guard positions or places to avoid or to find shelter was ideal.

Some of these items could be sent from London or Paris, but care had to be taken not to compromise the 'official' parcels sent by the Red Cross. The Germans became more vigilant as the war progressed and their searches became more thorough. A rubber pouch was found hidden in a jar of mixed pickles sent to an English officer in Holzminden camp. It contained forged rubber stamps as used by the police in the Leipzig and Aachen areas. Another parcel contained a gramophone in a box, modified with a false bottom and sides in which were hidden compasses, steel nibs and small bottles of ink. In the bottom were maps of the surrounding area up to the Dutch border, a disassembled wire-cutter and two small torches with spare batteries.

Advice was given such as to travel fourth-class on trains as it would be cheaper and with fewer controls; never offer one's seat to a lady; never speak unless it was absolutely necessary, irrespective of how well one could speak German; do not carry a bag in case a policeman asked to search it due to the illegal trade in food; carry a small amount of food wrapped in paper in one's hand; and, if caught, get rid of any maps and papers immediately.

The best way to travel was to avoid all towns, villages and people and to move only at night, finding a suitable place to hide before dawn. This would take time though, and the escapee would probably have to live off the land or from whatever food he managed to take with him. They were told to travel near to roads, but not actually on them and to beware of dogs around farms. Bridges were to be avoided as they were often guarded.

This part of the electrified fence along the German-Dutch border has claimed a victim. Guards from both countries wait for the power to be turned off before the victim can be recovered.

One prisoner who managed to escape to neutral Holland was a French NCO by the name of Jean Martin who reached safety in Holland in July 1915.

Corporal Jean Martin was a section leader in the French army who was hit by a shell burst during the retreat through Belgium. His comrades dressed the wound in his stomach and left him as the Germans got nearer. One of the enemy prepared to finish him off with his rifle butt, but another stopped him and knelt down to give him a drink of water instead. They then moved on. Later a German patrol searched him and took most of the food in his pack, leaving some bread and chocolate within reach.

Night fell and a German with a torch and a revolver found him and examined his wounds. He told him that he would be taken to hospital and went away. Martin heard revolver shots now and then in the night and assumed that it was the gravely wounded being given the final *coup de grâce*. It was broad daylight when stretcher-bearers arrived to take him away to a temporary hospital in a nearby castle.

The German doctor was a cheerful fellow and he treated both wounded Germans and French equally well and Martin's wound was attended to. The following day he was transported with other wounded Frenchmen to Fourmies station where he was lucky to receive coffee and bread and butter from a priest and sisters ministering to the wounded. Many of his comrades were loaded into a wagon used for transporting horses, but Martin and two others were sat in a third-class compartment with a guard. The Germans had been celebrating the night before and many were still drunk. One of Martin's comrades produced a bottle of champagne that he had liberated and they consumed their first liquid in two days.

Martin and the other French prisoners finally reached their prison camp, a German army barracks, and had to dig holes in the sand and cover them with branches as there was no accommodation for them. Eventually tents would be provided and later, after a visit from the American consul, they would be moved into stables, just vacated by their previous four-legged occupants.

Spring 1915 arrived and Martin's thoughts turned to escape. In April he had been moved from his original camp 150 kilometres from the border with Holland to one much nearer. At that time NCOs were not required to go out on working parties but it was the only way to spy out the lie of the land, to see how the sentries guarded the camp and what civilians were in the area to avoid. Together with five other NCOs, Martin exchanged his coat for one without stripes of rank and joined a fatigue party going to work in a saw mill. On the way they passed a bridge from which two prisoners had previously jumped into the river to escape. However, they could not swim and one drowned and the other was recaptured and beaten to death. Martin realized that he had to bide his time, for failure could mean the end of him.

There was no way to escape from the main camp, with its electrified fence and armed sentries. The only way to go was to abscond from one of the work parties. He went out several times and learned that there were no able-bodied men under 50 in the area and that the railways and bridges were guarded by the Germans. Civilian clothes were essential, but any such clothing received from France was modified before being given to the recipient. A large strip of cloth would be cut away and a wide coloured stripe sewn in its place to indicate that the wearer was a prisoner of war.

Eventually Martin was assigned to a party of forty men to be employed as wood-cutters. On the day that he escaped he waited until the sentries had eaten their midday meal and were lying down in the sun, and he crawled away into a nearby hollow. Now out of sight, he removed his

The electrified fence erected along the border with Holland.`

army jacket and tore the stripes from his trouser legs. He had acquired a thin cotton coat to go with the waistcoat that he already possessed and a cap made out of worn-out clothes and these he wore under his uniform. Now dressed as a civilian, he simply walked away from the working party and headed west.

In conversation with the guards, Martin had discovered a number of things that would be of use to him. He found out that the frontier was a mere 12 kilometres away as the crow flies. News of his escape would be transmitted all over the area by 150 telegrams and three battalions of *Landsturm* would be mobilized to search for him. A search party would be sent out using bloodhounds to follow his trail, and a sum of money would be promised to any civilian who took him into custody. The punishment for escaping would be forty-two days' solitary confinement, during which time he would receive only one meal every two days. That is, of course, if his captors did not shoot him out of hand when they finally caught up with him.

All of these thoughts would have been in Martin's head as he walked through the night, finding his way through two thick woods before seeking shelter in a dried-up stream bed as daylight approached. He spent a miserable day being plagued by mosquitos and a two-hour rainstorm left him soaked by the time darkness fell again. He did not make much progress the second night, having to take care to avoid nocturnal civilians, and in the distance he could hear searchers, firing blank rounds into bushes as they sought the escaper.

After a damp and miserable day spent hiding in a thicket and suffering from thirst, Martin continued his journey, guided by the Polar Star. He managed to avoid villages and farmhouses but the meadows and cornfields were full of noises that brought him to a halt, only to discover a lone cow or a flock of pheasants. As dawn approached he found a shallow stream which he

A typical French prisoner-of-war working party on a farm. Often the guards were less than vigilant and a determined escaper would often find an opportunity to slip away.

crossed, slaking his thirst for the first time in forty-eight hours. Suddenly he heard the sound of a German bugle playing reveille; a barracks not far away. He later wrote:

> An indescribable terror took possession of me, and I felt that I was going to be caught. A hundred metres farther on a stream barred my way; there was no possibility of hesitating, and so, at four o'clock in the morning, without taking time to remove any of my clothes, I plunged in. I was out of my depth almost immediately, and swam to the opposite bank, a distance of about forty metres.

Soaked to the skin and with the sun coming up over the horizon, Martin sought shelter in the open countryside. He carefully made his way into the middle of a cornfield and lay down. Before long he could hear peasants working in neighbouring fields and the sound of the German troops singing as they left their barracks to continue their search. It was clear that the searchers were now in the neighbourhood as he could hear the sound of dogs and occasional shots being fired. He decided to stay where he was that night and all the next day.

Fatigue was starting to overwhelm Martin, but he forced himself to carry on through his fourth night on the run. He was now passing the outskirts of a village, 3 kilometres from the frontier, and trying hard to appear as if he belonged there, even exchanging the occasional '*Guten Morgen*' with the odd civilian or sentry.

By six o'clock in the morning Martin had reached a crossroads with an empty sentry box in the middle. He hurried on through the meadows, searching for the river that would be his final obstacle to freedom. His strength was failing him now, but the sight of cavalrymen's helmets in the distance drove him forward and before he realized it he was standing on the bank of the river marked by neutral border posts. On the other side of the river stood a ferryman's house and he hailed him and waved him over. Within minutes he was in a small boat being rowed by an old Dutchman who would not accept any payment. Finally he stepped ashore in neutral Holland, safe at last. For his efforts he would later be awarded the Croix de Guerre and promoted to sergeant major.

French escaper Jean Martin walked away from his working party.

Another very enterprising escaper was 47-year-old Major Peter Anderson, who was attached to the 3rd Battalion, Canadian Infantry as chief scout to the 18th Brigade. Born in Denmark but living in Canada when war broke out, he was taken prisoner on 24 April 1915 outside St. Julien at the Second Battle of Ypres and was first taken to Roulers, where he was quite well treated. The Germans had taken many wounded prisoners as well as the major, who had been knocked out by an explosion, but they were left behind. As they were never heard from again, it is probable that the Germans killed them or left them to die. From Roulers he was taken via Louvain and Cologne to Bischofswerda in Saxony. The small town east of Dresden had a population of 8,000 and was under the jurisdiction of the 12th Army Corps. The officers' camp was in a new cavalry barracks situated some distance from the town, on a hill near some pine woods. The major later reported:

> The officer in charge of the train put us in a 4th Class carriage with some gassed Algerian troops. At Cassel a general asked him why he had put English officers with Algerian troops and he said he thought the Algerians were also officers. After that the Algerians were moved. The journey took three days and we were only given a little bread and water. I saw none of the German Red Cross. The guards treated us quite well, and at one place some of them got us beer. At most of the places we stopped at, the populace was either very hostile or indifferent. A good many of the Saxons like the English better than they like the Prussians. On the whole we were treated badly on the journey.

Major Anderson considered Bischofswerda to be the best prison camp in Germany. There were around 300 prisoners, including 40 British officers, 68 French, 7 Belgians and many Russians. The camp had never been used before and certainly not by prisoners. The larger rooms had

Bischofswerda prisoner of war camp in 1915, considered by Major Anderson to be the best prison camp in Germany.

been divided by temporary partitions, stoves had been installed and the regular rooms were all steam-heated. There were hot and cold baths for daily use and three tennis courts. They were able to play clock golf and baseball and had 4 acres of grounds for exercise, as well as a library of 2,000 books. There were up to a dozen officers in each room, although Anderson and Captain Straight had one to themselves. They had proper beds and bedding and orderlies drawn from the other rank prisoners to wait on them. Roll call was at 9 am and 5.20 pm.

The food was fair for prisoners of war and the quantities more than adequate. In the morning they had a white roll and weak coffee; in the middle of the day there was a substantial soup, meat and potatoes and the same in the evening. Extras could be purchased at a very reasonable price at the canteen, run by a Frau Moller who was very good at obtaining extras such as ink. A good beefsteak, onions and potatoes cost 1 mark, 20 pfennigs and five bottles of beer 1 mark. His pay as a major was 100 marks per month and he had to pay 50 of them per month for his food.

Despite the comfy conditions, Anderson knew where his duty lay and escaped on 28 September, having been in the camp exactly five months. It had taken him about three months to get ready: he needed to get his boots soled; to obtain new long trousers to replace his riding breeches; to acquire scissors, needle and thread, a rubber sponge bag for money, maps, matches, etc. and a rubber air cushion for crossing rivers. He also had to stockpile bread, meat lozenges, chocolate and biscuits and a German pipe and rucksack.

Two Australian and one Belgian officer in Karlsruhe officers' camp. (*Australian War Memorial*)

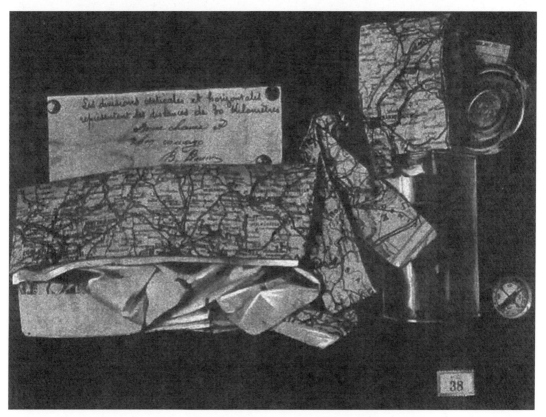

An escape kit including maps and compass sealed in a tin supposedly containing food.

A hand-drawn escape map. Even if escapers were recaptured and returned to their camp, they always learned something about the locality that could be used to update maps in the camp.

Back in England in November he wrote:

Escaping was very difficult, it took me seven hours to get out of the camp. There were three high wire fences and two rows of sentries with fixed bayonets. I left a letter behind addressed to the Commandant, Captain Eibenstein, stating that I had not been helped by any of my own comrades or by any of the officials of the camp, as I did not want to get them into trouble. The Commandant was quite a nice man; he had a glass factory in Bischofswerda. Sometimes he got drunk, on one occasion wanting to have a roll call in the middle of the night.

The English interpreter was a Prussian, not good, until we got him into a row with the Commandant and then he behaved better. He was very lazy, and often, instead of censoring our letters, he destroyed them. I was about 30 letters short. We were allowed to write two letters and four postcards per month and could receive any quantity. They tried to stop the letters for a time, but there was such a row about it that they had to give in.

Some officers were sent on to us at Bischofswerda from Konigstein and Munden. Konigstein was a fortress above the River Elbe and Munden was a factory building containing as many as 600 officers at a time. They reported that they had not been at all well treated and some had tried to escape from Munden, but were captured and placed in solitary confinement on bread and water for three months. A good many tried to escape all over Germany, but nearly all got shot, wounded and a few recaptured unwounded.

We were forbidden to speak to the guards, but sometimes we managed to do so and would give them cigarettes. In that way we would discover snippets that would help us with our escape plans. When escaping through Germany I passed as a Swede. The whole nation is in mourning, but confident. I was told that some time in June Leipzig had been under martial law and two newspapers suppressed. The German individual is not a fighting man, but organisation and discipline have been brought to the highest possible pitch. Their confidence has not yet been shaken and they think everything is going all right, but you never see a smile on any face, and after 9.30 at night no one is in the streets, everywhere deserted. They are all making the best of their resources, ploughing and seeding going on up to time, mostly done by women.

I do not think there are any small camps in Germany that we do not know of. The Germans seem just as anxious to find out about the missing as we are. I came back through Frankfurt, Berlin, Hamburg, Denmark, Sweden and Norway by ship from Bergen to Newcastle on Tyne. At the frontier the sentries were only four deep, although several mainly Russians got shot trying to cross into Denmark.

Major Anderson later wrote a letter to the camp commandant:

My Dear Old Commendant by force of Circumstances:-
It was on April 24, 1915 that I was taken Prisoner at Ypres after every man that was with me was killed. I was blown up twice and when I woke up I was a Prisoner. I arrived at your Hotel on 28th of April and it is no doubt one of the best, if not the best Prison Camp in Germany. I told them in the War Office in London that I believe I was in the Best Prison Camp in Germany.

But I could not resist the call of the wilds or wide spaces. While your camp was quite alright under the circumstances, there was not enough elbow room for me. I went to the war to fight my countries enemies and not to sit in a prison camp idly till the war was over.

There was nothing you could have done to keep me there. I had several different plans to get out and they were all practical. No one ever had a prison camp but there is always some way of getting out. I had been a big game hunter all my life. I can go get the big bull moose, elk, deer, grizzly bear. That being the case, yours or anyone else's sentries are worth little or nothing as far as I am concerned. I am used to see without being seen – can't get lost, not if I tried. I always knew where I was night and day, while travelling through Germany by foot.

I took train at Guben to Frankfort a/o Berlin, Wittenberg, Hamburg, Flensburg, and walked from there to Kolding in Demark, then by train to Copenhagen to the British Embassy and later to London, England, via Sweden and Norway.

When I arrived at the war office, I had gathered enough military information while travelling through Germany to have saved Servia, but it was not acted on, and you know the result.

How did I get over the Frontier? Well, as I said before, a few sentries don't matter with me. I passed four and a wire entanglement. It was very dark and raining. They never saw or heard me. I nearly fell over the first sentry. After that I was more careful. It was at a

Major Peter Anderson, the only Canadian officer to escape and make it home during the First World War, together with his wife Mary and their children.

little town named Frorup where I crossed the border – no one heard or saw me, although I was but a few inches from every one of the four sentries.

In the morning, they must have known someone had gone through as I lost a pipe I had bought from one of the Mollers in the Canteen at Bischofswerda and an electric torch I bought in Flensberg. No doubt these articles were found in the wire entanglements in the morning.

It rained the whole time I travelled through Germany. I was wet to the skin for 10 1/2 days until I arrived in Denmark. I stayed in the woods in the daytime and travelled at night as far as Guben, where I bought a raincoat, an umbrella, a hat, gloves etc. After that I travelled by trains like a Gentleman.

Major Anderson passed away in 1945 aged 77.

Chapter 10

Allied Prisoners of War

While this book deals mainly with allied prisoners of war on the Western Front, one should not neglect the vast numbers of prisoners taken by both sides on the Eastern Front. The statistics involved are enormous. Russia called to arms 16 million men, Germany 9 million, France 8.5 million, Great Britain 9 million, Italy 5.5 million and Austro–Hungary 9 million. The fighting that took place in the east between the Baltic and the Black Sea led to vast numbers of captives being taken on both sides. As early as September 1914 the Austro-Hungarian army lost 100,000 men taken prisoner out of the three-quarters of a million men committed to operations on the north-eastern front. When the Przemysl fortress fell on 23 March 1915, 9 generals, 2,600 officers and 117,000 soldiers fell into Russian hands. On the other side of the coin, at the Battle of Tannenberg at the end of August 1914, 100,000 Russians fell into German hands, and as the conquest of the Polish territories continued, the numbers of Russian prisoners of war rose. In August 1915 alone, some 325,000 Russians were taken prisoner by German and Austro-Hungarian forces.

It is estimated that 2.5 million Russian prisoners of war were taken, while 2 million Austro-Hungarians and 160,000 Germans fell into Russian hands. In addition, 600,000 Italians were taken prisoner by the Central Powers of Germany and Austro-Hungary. Of the prisoners held by the Russians, the mortality rates were also high, especially in the Siberian camps. Several hundred thousand soldiers of the Central Powers perished in Russian hands.

Austria-Hungary also found itself with over a million allied prisoners of war. The majority of them were Russians, but there were also Romanian, Serbian and Italian prisoners. More than 800,000 of them were incarcerated in Austrian prisoner-of-war camps, while the Hungarians had around 200,000 to deal with. Most of these arrived in the first year of the war during campaigns in Poland and on the Carpathian front. The numbers increased as the Central Powers advanced eastwards, until in March 1918 the Treaty of Brest-Litovsk was signed, ending the war with Russia.

The successful Austrian-German-Bulgarian offensive against Serbia in October 1915 resulted in large numbers of Serbs falling 'in the bag' and they were joined by large numbers of Romanians after that government declared war on Austria-Hungary in August 1916. They also took some 300,000 Italian prisoners of war towards the end of 1917, following the Battle of Caporetto in the October as they advanced into north-eastern Italy.

These camps were built to house prisoners on a massive scale and each held from 40,000 to 100,000 inmates. Rather than use existing barracks and buildings, they built most of them from scratch. Prisoner-of-war labour was used and conditions were harsh as the prisoners struggled to build their own accommodation.

Civilian prisons were also established, although these were generally smaller than their military counterparts and they were run by the Ministry of the Interior rather than the Ministry of War. In the dual Austro-Hungarian monarchy the two prisoner-of-war camp systems were

A group of French, British and Belgian prisoners of war at Döberitz camp.

A group of Russian prisoners of war at Döberitz camp.

Russian prisoners at Sprottau camp in Lower Silesia, Poland. Nearby was a barracks for TB patients.

Various types of Russian prisoners in the camp at Schneidemühl. The camp capacity was between 40,000 and 50,000, although many were out on working parties. The barracks were of the earthen type.

French prisoners in front of the kitchen at Kaltenkirchen camp.

Belgian prisoners in front of their kitchen at Kaltenkirchen camp.

A group of English prisoners at Wahn, situated 20 miles south-east of Cologne in the former Wahner Heide artillery training camp. There were 35,000 men on its books, including a barracks for prisoners caught trying to cross the frontier.

kept separate; one for the Austrian Empire and one for the kingdom of Hungary. The Austrians had the greater number of prison camps; twenty-eight main camps in five army corps districts. As in Germany, the camp commanders reported directly to the army corps commanders.

In Hungary there were eleven *Stammlagers* (the full version of 'stalag'), located in the 4th, 5th and 6th Army Districts and one in the 7th Army Corps region. Unlike the Austrians, the Hungarian camp commanders reported to the same headquarters at the 5th Army Corps at Pozsony.

The 10th Department of the Austro-Hungarian Ministry of War was responsible for all matters concerning prisoners of war. They were totally unprepared for the initial 200,000 prisoners that fell into their hands and immediately began construction of fifty prisoner-of-war camps, most of which were situated in what is now the Czech Republic. However, they underestimated the sanitary and hygiene requirements for the large camps and typhus epidemics swept through these in the winter of 1914–15. In the Mauthausen camp several thousand Serbian soldiers died in the early months of the war.

The largest Austro-Hungarian camp was Heinrichsgrun, which contained 30,000 Serbs, Russians and Italians. Forty men died each day from exhaustion and epidemics and 4,000 prisoners of war were buried in the camp cemetery. Most of these cemeteries would be abandoned at the end of the war and many have remained derelict ever since.

All participants in the war found that it was costly to keep all their prisoners in dedicated camps. Manpower was short due to military mobilization, so the working party system was developed in which labour detachments would be sent out to help the economy. Men would work on farms and in factories and mines, where they would at least be productive and could be fed locally. Unlike the British and French, the Russian, Serbian and Romanian prisoners suffered from a lack of food parcels from home. Italian prisoners fared better until the Caporetto disaster in late 1917 when huge numbers surrendered to the Austro-German forces.

Russian and French prisoners at Langensalza administered by the 11th Army Corps. The men were quartered in huts holding 250 men and many were sent out on working parties.

A selection of the various nationalities at Sagan camp, built on a flat sandy plain surrounded by forests. Shown are a Pole, two Russians, one Algerian, one Frenchman, one Caucasian and a Tartar.

Muslim prisoners at Wünsdorf, the Halbmondlager (crescent moon prisoner-of-war camp). In July 1915 the Germans opened the first mosque to be built on German soil for the prisoners.

Hindu prisoners of war suffered more than others in the harsh German winters.

Hindu prisoners of war in an unknown camp.

Hindu prisoners of war playing cards.

A potato-seller in Cassel, the headquarters of the 11th Army Corps and a town with a population of 153,000 souls. The 20,000 prisoners were employed in factories and workshops.

A French prisoner enjoying his pipe at Langensalza camp.

A Korean cook, one of the residents of the Danzig-Troyl camp. Danzig was the capital of West Prussia and the home of the 17th Army Corps who administered the camp.

Right: The caption for this picture of French and English prisoners at Ohrdruf camp was 'Entente Cordiale', so-named after a series of agreements signed in 1904 to improve Anglo-French relations.

Below: A group of officers at the officer camp at Halle on the River Saale. The prison camp for officers was in a disused factory built around three sides of a square.

An officer in his room at the camp at Werl, a Franciscan monastery built in 1913.

Seven Russian children prisoners of war with their German teacher. They served in the Russian army as orderlies or kitchen boys.

A diminutive Russian prisoner and his rather large jailer at Puchheim, just outside Munich in the south of Germany.

An unusual photograph of a female Cossack from the Don in male attire, who accompanied her husband to the war, now together at Hammerstein camp in West Prussia.

At Friedrichsfeld camp, a photograph captioned by the Germans as 'Champions of civilization from all countries'.

French Colonial troops from Senegal, Somalia, Guinea, Tunisia and Sudan.

Thereafter the Italian government branded these prisoners as deserters and cut off food parcel shipments.

The Germans concluded their book *1915* with an examination of the different nationalities in their custody. It makes interesting reading and helps us to understand the mentality of the Germans and their attitude towards 'racially inferior' countries:

Types of Nations

The present German prisoner of war camps, truly, afford a splendid opportunity for anthropological studies and research. A series of photographs show the enemies of Germany, partly in groups, partly in examples of the 'Entente Cordiale', a very popular motive for photography in the camps, one of which also forms the frontispiece of this booklet. The French and English were not always very pleased to come into such close contact with their Russian allies. Our pictures show the great differences existing amongst them. The next photograph is one characteristic of Russian types. Partly able-bodied men with clever features, partly men of a physique far inferior to that of the German troops, and with dull physiognomy. The Mongole type may be observed with quite a large number of Russian prisoners. But also the groups of French and Belgian prisoners from Kaltenkirchen and English prisoners from Wahn are characteristic. The photograph from the camp at Langensalza shows that the allies at least met for being photographed in camp. The photograph from Sagan comprises one Pole, two Russians, one Algerian, one Frenchman, one Caucasian and one Tartar. The following illustrations show the world of the Islam, the men hailing from the North of Africa or India, respectively.

The tradesman from the East cannot cast off his trade instinct even in the prisoners' camp, and the cheerful potato seller in our picture surely finds many a customer for sake of his cheerful mien alone. The typical Frenchman is as interesting a type as the Korean cook. A handsome group 'Entente Cordiale' is the one from Ohrdruf. The group from the officers' camp at Halle and the single photograph from Werl show that the appearance of the officers gives no reason for complaint.

Amongst the Russian prisoners a number of boys, ranging from 12 to 15 years were found, having served as orderlies and kitchen boys. Seven of these are seen in our picture together with their German teacher. The photograph from Puchheim shows that these boys found particular friends amongst the German officers. A quite exceptional photograph is that of a female Cossack from the Don in male attire, who accompanied her husband to the war. And lastly the photograph from Wesel shows us a mixed gathering of types and uniforms.

The following 14 photographs, forming the conclusion, show us, to use the words of Frederick the Great, with 'what sort of vagabonds Germany has to fight' and what the 'Champions for Liberty and Civilisation' bring forth to fight the 'German Huns'. It is with bitterness and rage that one considers how many a highly educated, promising German soldier and patriot lost his life by the rifle or even the knife of these hordes. The judgement of all justly thinking civilized nations of the world, and History will have to decide, how France and Great Britain may answer for how (if all had turned out to their intent) these fellows would have overrun the flourishing German lands and cast European civilisation backwards over a period of thousands of years.

A few samples of letters from prisoners of war, taken from many hundred thousands of similar ones, may in conclusion serve to show what these prisoners think and have to say of the treatment they receive in Germany:

Arsene D. to M. Bertin D:
.... Since I have been in Heiligenstadt, I have gained eight pounds in weight. We are well fed, receiving five meals a day. The cooking is done by Catholic nuns. From time to time a teacher, who knows France, and particularly the district of Arras, well, holds a discourse in French. All this is a welcome pastime for us.

Omer N. to Mdlle. Maria P:
I am quite changed. Before the war I weighed 120 pounds, now I weigh 140 pounds. I have always been perfectly well. I have now gone to work. I have good food and a good bed and am quite happy.

Belgian prisoner of war Michiel G to his brother:
I have grown a little fatter from the good life. I always still work at the office. We are treated very well and I am personally well and respected.

E.J. Russian prisoner. Village P. Gouvern. Volodga:
We are here treated very well, by no means as enemies, but as comrades. We indeed receive only three quarters of a pound of bread daily, but if Germany had more bread at her disposal, we surely would get more.

Charles R. to his parents:
Immediately after we were taken prisoners the German soldiers gave us cigarettes, cigars, coffee etc and we were treated, during transport, in the same manner, without the least brutality, as some people reported. We sleep on mattresses in huts. As regards the food, there is no cause for complaint.

Robert F. to his wife:
.... We are well treated. The Germans are not as bad as the newspapers say. Do not trouble, I am safe from bullets and guns, and sleep very calmly.

Alain L., 4th September 1915:
In fact I have not much to complain of, as today it is just one year that I boarded train at Cambray for transport into captivity. I had myself weighed at the time in the station and weighed, fully dressed, 118 pounds and today I am fatter than I ever was.

Gabriel R. to Mdme R. Widow:
We are very well treated, and the civilians show no hostile feeling against us; on the contrary, we are objects of their interest, and our boots clatter on the handsome, shady and well paved streets of Gottingen without any unfriendly murmuring being heard.

Joseph R:
My dear little wife. I must tell you that I am very well fed. I am in want of nothing. I work every day, earn 80 Pfennigs and am satisfied.

Alphonse M. to his wife:
.... Do not trouble for my sake, for I am very well. We receive good food, are fairly well paid, and I ask you to send news concerning me through Albertine to Maurice and to tell him, that I am very well off, and that I wish, he were with me.

Private D. to his wife:
.... I am working here on a farm and receive ample food, so that it is not necessary for you, to send me any further bread or money.

The reader might compare these letters and the above photographs with the constant reports in French and English papers, relating of the inhuman treatment of the prisoners of war in Germany. In view of such facts, we may neglect the occurrence that from time to time some prisoner of war writes a letter home full of complaints. It will never be possible to fully satisfy, alone as regards the food, such a vast number as one and a half million individuals. Besides it has been proved in a Court Martial that a prisoner has admittedly reported falsely, in order that his people at home should send him as many comforts as possible.

Germany's Emperor, Government and People did not want the war, but when it was enforced upon them, they have bravely defended themselves and waged it both in the field and at home with a thorough organisation and active deeds. Both the vast number of prisoners of war, and also their treatment will form a glorious leaf in the War History of the German Empire.

Postscript

The majority of the prisoners taken during the war fell in the bag at the beginning and towards the end when the arrival of American troops began to tip the balance in the allies' favour. In between, the vast lines of trenches were excavated and each side took turns in launching offensives that did little to hasten the end of the war. Eventually accommodation of a sort was provided for most prisoners and large numbers of work parties were formed to replace the labour lost as the Germans conscripted more and more men into the army. Food would become more scarce as the war progressed and the prisoners would suffer accordingly. Parcels from home and from the Red Cross could mean the difference between life and death. However, among the prisoner population there were men who refused to accept their predicament and who considered it their duty to try to escape. The stories of some of these men and their efforts to escape from captivity will be described in Book Two, *The Kaiser's Escapees*, due for publication in 2018.

Index